Syntactic and Semantic Mastery of English Auxiliaries by Kurd Learners at College Level

Paiman Hama Salih Sabir

University Press of America,® Inc.
Lanham • Boulder • New York • Toronto • Plymouth, UK

Copyright © 2016 by University Press of America,® Inc.
4501 Forbes Boulevard, Suite 200, Lanham, Maryland 20706
UPA Acquisitions Department (301) 459-3366

Unit A, Whitacre Mews, 26-34 Stannary Street,
London SE11 4AB, United Kingdom

All rights reserved
Printed in the United States of America
British Library Cataloguing in Publication Information Available

Library of Congress Control Number: 2015946978
ISBN: 978-0-7618-6655-8 (pbk : alk. paper)—ISBN: 978-0-7618-6654-1 (electronic)

∞™ The paper used in this publication meets the minimum requirements of American National Standard for Information Sciences Permanence of Paper for Printed Library Materials, ANSI/NISO Z39.48-1992.

To the pure soul of my father
To my mother
To my faithful brothers and sisters

Contents

List of Figures	ix
List of Tables	xi
Acknowledgments	xiii
Abbreviations	xv
Kurdish Phonemic System	xvii

1 Introduction 1
   1.1 The Problem 1
   1.2 Aims of the Study 2
   1.3 Hypotheses of the Study 2
   1.4 The Procedures 3
   1.5 Delimitation 3
   1.6 Value of the Study 4

2 Central Concepts in Foreign Language Learning 5
   2.1 Foreign Language and Second Language 5
   2.2 Acquisition 5
   2.3 Language Learning 6
   2.4 Hypotheses Explaining L1 and L2 Similarities/Differences 8
   2.5 Error Analysis 9
   2.6 Errors and Mistakes 9
   2.7 Transfer 12
   2.8 Interlanguage 13
   2.9 Factors on Second Language Acquisition (SLA) 14
   2.10 The Role of Social Context in Language Learning 19
   2.11 Learning Strategies 20

	2.12 The Role of Output in SLA	22
	2.13 Formal Instruction	22
	Notes	24
3	Auxiliary Verbs in English	25
	3.1 The Structure of the English Verb Phrase	25
	3.2 Auxiliary Verbs	26
	3.3 Functional Criteria for the Auxiliary verbs	29
	3.4 Syntactic Properties of Primary Aux. (Be, Do and Have)	30
	3.5 Modal Auxiliaries or the Modals	34
	3.6 Syntactic Features of Modal Auxiliaries	35
	3.7 Central Modal Auxiliaries	36
	3.8 Marginal Modal Auxiliaries	37
	3.9 Modal Idioms	39
	3.10 Semi-Auxiliaries	39
	3.11 Catenative-Verbs	40
	3.12 Order of Auxiliary Verbs	41
	3.13 Mood and Modality	41
	3.14 The Tri-Dimensionality of the Modals	43
	3.15 The Semantic Aspect of Auxiliary verbs	45
	3.16 Tense, Time and the Modals	50
	3.17 Two Different Treatments of Modal Meanings	52
	3.18 Auxiliaries in Kurdish	54
	3.19 Auxiliary Verbs in Kurdish: A Traditional Perspective	55
	3.20 Other Auxiliary Verbs	57
	3.21 Function of the Auxiliaries	59
	3.22 Mood	60
	3.23 Modality Expressions	61
	3.24 Modal Meanings	64
	Notes	68
4	Data Collection	71
	4.1 Test Design	71
	4.2 The Sample	72
	4.3 Test Objectives	72
	4.4 Test Merits	73
	4.5 Pilot Testing	75
	4.6 Selection of the Test Material	75
	4.7 Final Administration	76
	4.8 The Scoring Scheme	76
	4.9 Statistical Means	76
	Note	78
5	Data Analysis and Discussion of the Results	79
	5.1 Discussion of the Results	79

	5.2 Quantitative Assessment	79
	5.3 Factors behind Learners' Errors	82
	Notes	100
6	Conclusions, Pedagogical Recommendations and Suggestions for Further Research	101
	6.1 Conclusions	101
	6.2 Pedagogical Implications	102
	6.3 Suggestions for Further Research	103
Appendix		105
	The Test	105
Bibliography		109
	Interviews	113
About the Author		115

List of Figures

Fig. 5.1	Comparing correct responses of Q1 and Q2.	82
Fig. 5.2	Comparing recognition and production results.	88

List of Tables

Table 3.1	Modal Meanings.	65
Table 3.2	Kinds of Modality Expressed by the Lexical Modals.	66
Table 4.1	The Scoring Scheme	77
Table 5.1	Frequencies and Percentage of the Subjects' Performance Question (1)	80
Table 5.2	Frequency and Percentage of the Subjects' Performance Question (2)	81
Table 5.3	Summary Statistics of Q1 and Q2.	83
Table 5.4	Frequency and Percentage of the Subjects' Performance Question (3)	84
Table 5.5	Frequency and Percentage of the Subjects' Performance Question (4)	85
Table 5.6	Frequency and Percentage of the Subjects' Performance Question (5)	86
Table 5.7	Subjects' Whole Achievement at Both Levels	87
Table 5.8	Summary Statistics of Recognition and Production	89
Table 5.9	Errors with *do*	90
Table 5.10	Errors with *be*	91
Table 5.11	Errors with *have*	92
Table 5.12	Errors with the Modals	93

Table 5.13	Errors with the Modals (continued).	95
Table 5.14	Errors with the Modals (continued)	95
Table 5.15	*be* Redundancy (errors with the modals).	96
Table 5.16	Errors with the Modals (Continued).	96
Table 5.17	Mismatching of Auxiliary in Tags	97
Table 5.18	Confusion of Modal Meanings in the Recognition Level	99
Table 5.19	Confusion of Modal Meanings in the Production Level	99

Acknowledgments

First and foremost, my gratitude is addressed to Allah, the source of all knowledge and wisdom and best prayers and peace be upon His messenger Mohammed and his pure descendants.

I would like to express my gratitude and thanks to my supervisor Dr. Salah Mohammed Salih for his support and instructive suggestions throughout the preparation of this work.

Special thanks are due to my teachers in the M.A. course, who were also the source of co-operation and help in preparing this study.

Sincerest thanks are due to the jury members whom I contacted mainly via e-mail for establishing the validity of the test and their considerable suggestions.

Thanks are also due to the Dean, teaching staff and the students of the Department of English, in the Colleges of Languages and Basic Education of Saladin, Sulaimani and Koya for their cooperation in carrying out the test.

I am also greatly indebted to Dr. Mohammed Mahwi for his invaluable help and support that enriched my study with his explanations on Kurdish grammatical structure and to my ex-colleague Mr. Mu'ayad Tahseen, a lecturer at college of Arts, university of Mosul for his support, suggestions and encouragement.

My thanks are also due to Mr. Kawa Mohammed Jamal, a lecturer in the College of Commerce and Statics, University of Sulaimani who was most helpful in doing the statics for my study

Finally, I would like to express my sincerest thanks to my family especially my mother for their continuous support, patience and encouragement.

Abbreviations

AdjPs—Adjective Phrases
Advps—Adverb Phrases
C.V.—Coefficient Variation
CAH—Contrastive Analysis Hypothesis
EA—Error Analysis
ESL—English as a Second Language
EFL—English as a Foreign Language
FL—Foreign Language
FQ—Frequency
Inf.—Infinitive
L2—Second Language
LAD—Language Acquisition Device
MDH—Markedness Differential Hypothesis
NP—Noun Phrase
ND—No Date
NICE—Negating, Inversion, Code, Emphatic
NECI—New English Course For Iraq
PPS—Prepositional Phrases
Q—Question
SLA—Second Language Acquisition
SDRH—Similarity Differential Rate Hypothesis
SD—Standard Deviation
TL—Target Language
UG—Universal Grammar
VP—Verb Phrase
WFs—Weak Forms

Kurdish Phonemic System

/p/ voiceless bilabial stop, as in /pir/, old, /pšila/, cat, /ĉāp/, print.
/b/ voiced bilabial stop, as in /bir/think, /rŭbar/, river, /kteb/, book.
/t/ voiceless dental stop, as in /task/, tight, /xotan/, you, /xot/, yourself.
/d/ voiced dental stop, as in /dask/, handle, /badan/, body, /bard/, rock.
/k/ voiceless velar stop, as in /kār/, job, /ĉāka/, goodness, /pāk/, clean.
/g/ voiced velar stop, as in/gošt/, meat, /lagan/, vessel, /sag/, dog.
/q/ voiceless uvular stop, as in /qal/, crow, /pāqla/, bean, laq/, leg.
/f/ voiceless labiodental fricative, as in /fel̄/, trick, /bafir/, snow, /kaf/, foar.
/v/ voiceless labiodental fricative, as in /govār/, magazine, /mirov/, human.
/s/ voiceless dental sibilant, as in/swer/, salty, /māsī/, fish, /kas/, person.
/z/ voiced dental sibilant, as in zawa/, bridegroom, /harzān/, cheap, /barz/, high.
/š/ voiceless alveopalatal sibilant, as in /šer/, lion, /pāšā/, king, /bāš/, good.
/ž/ voiced alveopalatal sibilant, as in/ žer/, beneath, /šāžīn/, queen, /nwež/, prayer.
/x/ voiceless velar fricative, as in /xwā/, God, / baxit/, luck, /bāx/, garden.
/r/ voiced velar fricative, as in /rar/, run, /ara/, lord, /wil̄ār/, cattle.
/ĥ/ voiceless faucalized pharyncal fricative, as in /hawt/, seven, /zahmat/, trouble.
/?/ voiced faucalized pharyncal fricative, as in /?ayb/, shame, /sa?āt/, watch,/bā?/.
/h/ voiceless glottal fricative, as in /hāwre/, friend, / sahol̄/, ice, /gwnāh/, crime.

/ĉ/ voiceless alveopalatal affricate, as in /ĉwār/, four, /pārĉa/, piece, /kiĉ/, girl.
/j/ voiced alveopalatal affricate, as in / jwlaka/, jew, /hanjīr/, fig, /tāj/, crown.
/m/ voiced bilabial nasal, as in /min/, I, /āmāda/, ready, /kam/, little.
/n/ voiced dental nasal, as in /nān/, bread, /binešt/, gum, /bān/, roof.
/ŋ/ voiced velar nasal, as in /haŋgwīn/, honey, /bāŋ/, call.
/l/ voiced clear dental lateral, as in /lew/, lip, /kilīl/, key, /ĉil/, forty.
/ł/ voiced dark alveolar lateral, as in..../gŭłāw/,rose water, /gił/, soil.
/r/ voiced alveolar flap, as in /birin/, to wound, /kar/, donkey.
/r/ voiced alveolar trill, as in /rož/, day, /brin/, to cut, /kar/, deaf.
/w/ voiced labiovelar rounded glide, as in /wak/, like, / hāwīn/, summer, / nāw/, name.
/y/, voiced palatal glide, as in /yārī/, game, /bayān/, dawn, /kay/, when.
/ī/ high close front unrounded long vowel, as in /īš/, work, /žīn/, life, /sī/, thirty.
/i/ high open front unrounded short vowel, as in /žin/, woman...
/ē/ mid very close front unrounded long vowel, as in /ema/, we, /zer/, gold.
/û/ high close rounded long vowel, as in /žûr/, room, / dû/, two.
/u/ high open back rounded short vowel, as in /umed/, hope, /kun/, hole...
/o/ mid open back rounded short vowel, as in /oqra/, calm, / kon/, old, /bo/ ,why.
/ā/ low central unrounded long vowel, as in /āsmān/, /sky, /mār/, snake, / bā/, wind.
/a/ low central unrounded short vowel, as in /ark/, duty, /kar/, donkey.

Chapter One

Introduction

1.1 THE PROBLEM

In English, auxiliary verbs are a set of verbal group with certain formal features by which they are discriminated from lexical verbs. Auxiliaries are of two subtypes; primary and the modals. On one hand, *do, be and have* are the only primary auxiliaries in English that have distinct syntactic features. On the other hand, the modals are a closed class of verbs that are of great magnitude semantically; it is by virtue of the modals that speakers of English express different propositions and attitudes in their utterances.

It is observed that the auxiliary verbs (primary and the modals) are the source of difficulty for the majority of EFL learners with different language backgrounds such as Arabs, Indians and Chinese. Linguists and researchers such as Leech (1971); Celece- Murcia and Larsern-Freeman (1999); Chandra Bose (2005) have observed this fact. As far as the modal meanings, Leech (1971: 7) states that:

> Every language has its peculiar problems of meaning for the foreign learner; and most people would agree that in the English language, the most troublesome problems are concentrated in the area of the finite verb phrase, in particular, questions of tense, aspect, and modal auxiliary usage.

Kurd EFL learners are not exceptions, since they face problems with the meanings and use of the modals. Difficulties are ascribed to the following factors:

1. Recent research indicates that Kurdish language lacks modal verbs like those found in English in form and function (Bomba, 2001: 78–88) and (Ahmed, 2005: 6).

2. Another source of difficulty is the diversity of the forms of the modals. Central modals, for instance, are different within themselves in their past formation, *can* has *could* as an equivalent past form whereas the past form of *must* is *had to*. Moreover each subcategory of the modals has different syntactic behaviour. Consequently, learners may overgeneralize the rule for of one type of modal verb to another, for instance the rule for *may* to *must*.
3. The meanings of the modals are assumed to be another source of difficulty. Each modal can have more than one meaning and each meaning is a member of an inter-related system which in turn leads to confusion and ambiguity of use by the learner.

Moreover, Byrd (1995) points out that, "the problem lies not in the surface positioning of the modals nor in their wide range of meaning, but in associating the right modal with the right meaning", (cited in Harris, McLaughlin, Still, ND: 1).

To the best of the researcher's knowledge, no study has been attempted in this concern to gauge the Kurd EFL learners' potential ability in recognizing and producing English auxiliary verbs.

1.2 AIMS OF THE STUDY

This study aims at:

1. Identifying Kurd EFL university students' performance in recognizing and producing the syntactic and semantic aspects of English auxiliaries.
2. Assessing the students' errors according to the results obtained from the test and coming up with findings.
3. Finding out the reasons beyond students' errors and suitable suggestions to help Kurd EFL university students to overcome the problems in learning English auxiliary verbs.

1.3 HYPOTHESES OF THE STUDY

It is hypothesized that:

1. Most Kurd EFL university students do not have full mastery of English auxiliary verbs.
2. Kurd learners' ability in recognizing forms is anticipated to be better than their ability in recognizing meanings of English auxiliaries.

3. The performance of Kurd EFL university students at the recognition level is anticipated to be better than their performance at the production one.

1.4 THE PROCEDURES

In order to achieve the objectives of the study, the researcher adopts the following steps.

1. Introducing key terms and concepts, which are related to foreign language learning so that the reader would have an idea of them when they are used in the analysis of errors in chapter five.
2. Producing, as far as possible, a comprehensive and clear exposition of syntactic and semantic aspects of English auxiliaries depending on the literature available in this field to provide the reader an insight about the types, forms, and the syntactic and semantic functions of each class of auxiliaries in general and to individual auxiliary in the language.
3. Constructing and administrating a test to Kurd EFL university students to diagnose the problems they might face in using auxiliary verbs at the two levels; the syntactic and semantic.
4. Statically computing and analyzing the results of the test and conclusions thereupon will be drawn.

1.5 DELIMITATION

This study is limited to testing third year College students, Department of English, At Colleges of Languages in the Universities of Saladin, Sulaimani and Koya and in Colleges of Basic Education, University of Saladin and Sulaimani during the academic year (2007–2008).

Students of these three universities have been chosen as the sample of this study since all have similar Kurdish dialect background, which is the central dialect (Standard Sorani), while students of Duhok University are excluded as they speak Bādīnī, the Northern dialect. These two dialects are different in terms of the types of auxiliary verbs; hence, functions of the auxiliaries (see Marif, 2000: 267–270) and Baha'addin (1987: 232–235). Moreover, the third year students have been selected for two reasons: first, they were taught this topic during the second year of their study, second, they are at the advanced level.

1.6 VALUE OF THE STUDY

The findings of this study are hoped to be of value for syllabus designers, teachers and Kurd EFL learners, since the study is concerned with problems that Kurd EFL learners encounter in mastering English auxiliary verbs. Accordingly, remedial programs can be attempted in such a way to help Kurd EFL learners master this problematic area of the language.

Chapter Two

Central Concepts in Foreign Language Learning

2.1 FOREIGN LANGUAGE AND SECOND LANGUAGE

Generally, the terms *foreign language* and *second language* are used in association with the geographical context where a language is spoken. On one hand, the term foreign language comprises the language which has neither local use in commerce, administration and education nor has immediate native speakers, (Johnson and Johnson, 1999: 133). It applies to any language other than the learner's mother tongue as it is defined in the Encyclopedia of English Language, "A language which is not the mother tongue of a speaker is a foreign language", (Crystal, 2004: 462). On the other hand, the language which is usually used within the community or regional area for communication and has official status is known as a second language (henceforth, L2).

2.2 ACQUISITION

Acquisition is a natural, unconscious and unplanned process that occurs without direct instruction or conscious focus on linguistic forms or feedback. This term was basically used to refer to the acquisition of the mother tongue by children and labeled as *First Language Acquisition* (henceforth, L1). Later, it came to cover both child and adult language learning, as adults are thought to undergo a similar process of acquisition especially in bilingual communities. But some other researchers confine it to the L2 scope. Ellis (1985: 292) assures that acquisition refers to "the internalization of rules and formulas which are then used to communicate in the second language".

A number of theories and models have been developed in terms of explanation of language acquisition. They differ in terms of internal and external factors involved in the process. For the behaviourists acquisition occurs via imitation and consolidated by correction and feedback, whereas for the mentalists, who oppose the former approach, acquisition is based on the existence of special modules in the mind containing innate knowledge and principles common to all languages. Finally, the functionalists language is contextually based, since they believe that children learn underlying structures but not superficial word order.

All these controversial assumptions rise from the complexity of human brain and its abstractness, which can not be accessed indirectly via performance.

2.3 LANGUAGE LEARNING

Language learning can be described as a conscious, formal and planned process, in which the FL learner is aware of the rules of the language he is learning. It is characterized by feedback and rule isolation. Brown (1994: 205) states that learning differs from acquisition in its trial-and-error nature. It also varies in order, i.e., not all learners learn alike, and can be used by learners who are in their teens, i.e., they can comprehend grammatical rules in this age.

Learning has been described differently in accordance with different approaches. For the behaviourists, it is "acquiring the ability to use its structure within a general vocabulary under essentially the conditions of normal communication among native speakers at normal conversational speed." (Lado, 1964: 38). In other words, it means "learning the expression, the content, and their association for rapid use in the proper positions within the system of the target language", (ibid.). On the other hand, it is as Long finds it "ability to improve L2 performance in language like performance in general," (cited in Spolsky 1989: 97). According to Oxford Learners' Dictionary (1989: 710) it is "a knowledge obtained by study".

Cognitive psychologists claim that learning requires attention and effort. Some information theorists argue that learning a language is like any skill acquired via intentional learning and then through practice it turns into automatic. In this respect, learning can be viewed as "the movement from controlled to automatic processing via practice" (Mitchell and Myles, 2004: 101). Similarly, Kimble and Garmezy point out that "Learning is a relatively permanent change in behavioural tendency and is the result of reinforced practice", (cited in Brown, 1994: 7).

The traditional view on learning is that the younger one starts to learn a second language, the better chance for success he has. Though Spolsky

(1989: 96) has the same view, recent researches show that the younger-the-better principle is only valid in environments where there is constant and natural exposure to L2, (Cohen and Dornyei, 2002: 171). Ellis (1985: 108) points out that younger learners succeed in pronunciation more than on other linguistic scales. Furthermore, Snow and Hoenfnagel-Hohel (1978) indicate that "adolescent and young adult L2 learners are faster in initial stages of L2 learning than young children . . . on all linguistic measures 'SYNTAX, MORPHOLOGY, PRONUNCIATION, LEXIS", (cited in Johnson and Johnson, 1999: 7).

As for Krashen's monitor theory-acquisition / learning hypothesis, learning "comprises a conscious process which results in conscious knowledge 'about' the language, for example knowledge of grammar rules" (cited in Schütz, 2005: 2). Moreover, he sees these two processes independent and that acquired knowledge involves subconscious FL rules that the learner calls upon automatically whereas the learned knowledge consists metalingual knowledge. This knowledge works only as a monitor before or after the utterance being produced that may alter the output of the acquired knowledge.

Based on Krashen's assumption, Widdowson (1990: 20) conceives of language learning as:

> The process of conscious intervention whereby performance initiated by the natural and unconscious process of acquisition is monitored, so that elements which have been leaned as formal rules are grafted on the elements which emerge spontaneously from the domain of the unconscious.

Johnson and Johnson (1999: 135) postulate two types of language learning: *natural and formal*. Other researchers use other terms, like *untutored and tutored*, *spontaneous and classroom* learning for this classification. *Untutored* or natural learning is that in which the FL is picked up in an unconstrained environment, where variety of styles characterized as (free and normal) are in use, with the communication purpose. In naturalistic environments FL learners are exposed to the FL as it is spoken by native speakers. As for *tutored or formal learning*, it occurs in a situation where only one person has command of it, the form of input is simplified, controlled, modified (bookish) and selective; more than these, the learning time is limited. This sort of learning is roughly known as *classroom learning*.

Nowadays, however, researchers on Second Language Acquisition (henceforth, SLA) use acquisition as a cover term to refer both to acquisition of a L1 by children and to the learning of further languages or varieties as it was hinted at (in the acquisition definition). Crystal (1992: 5), for example, defines acquisition as "the process or result of learning a particular aspect of language, or the language as a whole". The term is used with reference both to the learning of L1 by children or to the learning of further languages or varieties.

2.4 HYPOTHESES EXPLAINING L1 AND L2 SIMILARITIES/DIFFERENCES

When a language learner learns a second language, he has already some knowledge of his first language (or mother tongue). Even the L1 acquirer presupposes some degree of 'innate language specific capacity represented by the UG' (Spolsky, 1989: 117).

Contrastive analysis hypothesis (henceforth, CAH) had a crucial impact on research in applied linguistics and language teaching in the heydays of the Audio-Lingual Method. Its task was to compare the structures of two languages and to point out the differences (the source of difficulty for the learner). After a period CAH lost its popularity and weakened. Spolsky (1989: 119) points to one of the reasons of this weakening as it is referred learners' errors to only one source, which is transfer. Moreover CAH could not give any explanation for the area of difficulty as Briere (1968) shows "difference by itself does not predict difficulty; often there is more difficulty in practice with structures that are similar than with structures that are different."(cited in Spolsky, 1989: 120)

Therefore, Oller and Ziahosseiny (1970) proposed a moderate version to account for the hierarchy of difficulty. Thus, "whenever patterns are minimally distinct in form or meaning in one or more systems, confusion may result." (Cited in Major and Kim, 1996: 467). This addition is made on the basis of their study on Japanese learners learning English script. Moreover other studies have been done in this to account like the one of Wode (1983a: 180) who incorporated the similarity / dissimilarity notion to claim that only those elements of L2 are substituted by L1 items that meet 'specifiable similarity requirements'(cited in Major and Kim, 1996: 468).

Eckman (1977) also made another attempt to refine CAH by incorporating in it some principles of UG. He argues that "one should be able to make statements that do not merely describe differences but also predict difficulty", (cited in Spolsky, 1989: 121). Thus, Eckman proposed the notion of markedness to 'define directionality of difficulty', (Brown, 1994: 202) and to explain 'different levels of proficiency and order of acquisition' (Major and Kim, 1996: 470). Eckman's hypothesis is known as Markedness Differential Hypothesis (henceforth, MDH): "less marked phenomenon are acquired before marked ones", (ibid, 1996: 470). Eckman (1977: 320) states this hypothesis in the form of a hierarchal relationship; "A phenomena A in some language is more marked than B; but if the presence of A in a language implies the presence of B; but the presence of B does not imply the presence of A", (cited in Spolsky, 1989: 122). This means that the presence of more marked phenomena implies the presence of less marked, but not vice versa.

Accordingly, MDH sheds light on the systematic comparisons of L1 and L2 and the universal markedness relations. It predicts that "areas of the target language that are more marked than the native language, will be more difficult, depending on the relative degree of marking, while difference in form without difference in marking will not cause difficulty", (ibid, 1989: 122).

There have been some developments of Eckman's proposal. Major and Kim (1996) put another hypothesis forward which is known as The Similarity/ Differential Rate Hypothesis (henceforth, SDRH): "an L2 phenomenon that is dissimilar to an L1 phenomenon is acquired faster than a L2 phenomenon that is similar to this same L1 phenomenon." (Major and Kim, 1996: 474). This hypothesis takes into account similarity/ differential rate of accusation whereas Eckman's takes markedness differentials. Moreover, this hypothesis claims that dissimilar phenomenon is acquired more quickly than the reverse (similar phenomenon), whereas markedness is a mediating factor; a greater degree of markedness will slow down rate of acquisition, i.e., the rate of acquisition for dissimilar phenomenon is faster than for similar phenomenon.

2.5 ERROR ANALYSIS

Error analysis (henceforth EA) is the behaviourist approach to the understanding of the foreign language which consists of a set of procedures for identifying, describing, explaining learner errors."(Ellis and Barkhuizen, 2005: 51). It is systematic investigation of learners errors that explores the source of errors is not only from the L1 as CAH (henceforth), but basis of the theories of L1 and FL learning and the similarities between them. EA "tries to account for learner performance in terms cognitive processes learners make use of in recognizing the input they receive from the target language", (Keshaverz, 2004: 50).

2.6 ERRORS AND MISTAKES

Errors and mistakes may seem to point to the same notion from the first glance, but in fact they are different. Generally, for Corder (1973: 260) they constitute a "breach of the rule of the code"[1]. Falk (1978: 360) sees them as "systematic deviations from the foreign language and are due to emerging system that the language learner is constructing". In addition, errors can be described as a linguistic form or a cluster of forms which are not produced by native speakers in the same context and under similar conditions of production. They are seen as unavoidable aspect in learning as people can not learn without first systematically committing errors. They refer to "those parts of conversation or composition that deviate from some selected norm of mature language performance", (Dulay, Burt and Krashen, 1982: 138). Brown (1994: 205) sees errors as "idiosyncrasies in the interlanguage of the learner that are direct manifestations of a system within which a learner is operating at the time".

Brown (1987: 211) indicates that learners make different types of errors in different stages of their L2 learning. Therefore, researchers identify several stages of learners' errors reflecting learners' interlanguage development. Accordingly, there are four stages of interlanguage. First, *random errors* or *pre-systematic*, the learner is not aware that certain class of items is systematic, for example (*He mays come). Second, *emergent stage*, the learner begins to discern a system and is able to correct his own errors. Third, *systematic*, the learner confidently corrects his errors and finally, *stabilization* stage, or *post-systematic*, in this stage the errors are few that they cannot be detected and the language system has been mastered well enough that the learner no longer waits for feed back from others any more,

In earlier works on SLA, like Dulay, Burt and Krashen (1982), five common error types have been recognized; omitting grammatical morphemes, regularizing rules, using archiforms, misordering. However, (Ellis and Barkhuizen, 2005: 56) state that only two types of errors have been pointed out: overt and covert errors. The former is that which can be detected by the sentence/utterance, whereas the latter appears when a larger stretch of discourse is taken into consideration. Sentence level and discourse level terms are often used instead.

Consequently, different sources of errors made by L2 learners, as findings on SLA indicate have been reported. According to Contrastive Analysis Hypothesis (henceforth, CAH), errors are the result of the differences between L1 and L2. Transfer is the sole source in this case. Whereas for another approach like Error Analysis (henceforth, EA) errors emerge out of variety of sources; L1 is one of the causes. Ellis and Barkhuizen (2005: 62) argue that they may arise because of the existence of gaps in the learners L2 knowledge. However, Brown (1994: 206) shows that other sources of errors have been identified despite interference which is known as interlingual errors of interference, interalingual errors within the target language which emerge from the psycholinguistic or cognitive strategies or from countless affective variables. Those strategies used by the learners in this respect are:

1. False analogy which is a kind of overgeneralization: for example: boy-boys, * child-childs.
2. Misanalysis: here learners assume, for example, that 'means' is plural because of (-s).
3. Incomplete rule application: it is a kind of undergeneralization, e.g.,

4. *Nobody know where was Ahmed.*
5. Exploiting redundancy: which is omitting grammatical features that do not participate in the meaning of the utterance, for example (3rd person singular s), e.g., * Alan like tennis.
6. Overlooking co-occurrence restriction, for instance, though knowing that quick and fast are synonyms, failing to recognize the quick food collocation is not possible.
7. Simplification: it refers to the substitution of two or more target language forms by a simple form in order to simplify the burden of learning for instance, 'that 'is used as 'ubiquitous pronoun', (ibid. 65). It involves also the omission of form words and affixes, like the omission of auxiliary (be): * *He studying now*.

Some other types of errors are natural or (induced errors or contextual) which result from the way that language taught, for example:
Teacher: younghee, ask Keiko where she went to school.
Sook: Keiko, *where you went to school? (ibid).

On the other hand *mistakes* are seen as "random deviations unrelated to any system and instead representing the same type of performance or writing of a native speaker" (Falk, 1978: 360), or as 'failure of performance' similar to those performance mistakes committed by native language speakers for example (slips of tongue or pen). There is also another type of mistakes indicated by Yule (1988) which is slip *of ear* that may provide some clues as how the brain tries to make sense of the auditory signal it receives. For example, one understands (great ape) for (*grey ape) or vice versa, (cited in Keshaverz, 2004: 50).

Distinguishing mistakes from errors is not an easy task. "Errors" are the result of the difficulty of processing forms that are fully mastered. "They are not physical failures but the sign of an imperfect knowledge of the code." (Corder, 1973: 259), whereas "mistakes" are the outcome of non-linguistic factors like memory limitation, strong emotion, fatigue, lack of concentration, etc, (ibid: 1973: 258). There are certain criteria for identifying errors. The general criterion for this distinction is the frequency of occurrence, i.e., errors of high frequency are considered as errors whereas those with low frequency are mistakes, (Keshaverz, 2004: 51).

However, other criteria are to ask the learner which processes they invoke when they are ignorant of the used target language form or forms. Another way is to check whether the learner alternates between the erroneous form and the target language form, if the learner could correct that deviant form by him/herself, in this case it would be classified as a mistake.

2.7 TRANSFER

Transfer is a general term, which describes the effect of one's native language on the newly acquired knowledge, i.e., L2 or foreign language. Dulay, Burt and Krashen point to three uses of this term. For the behaviourist psychologist it is used to refer to a "process described as the automatic, uncontrolled and subconscious use of past learned behaviours in the attempt to produce new responses", (Dulay, Burt and Krashen 1982: 100–101). In this sense two types of transfer have been recognized; positive and negative. Positive transfer occurs when the old habit or behaviour and the new habit (behaviour) were identical. In this case the old habit facilitates the formation of the new one and results in correct performance. Conversely, when the old and the new behaviour were different, negative transfer occurs and results in error, which is known by FL researchers as *interference*.

Educational psychologists and educators have used this term to describe the use of 'past knowledge or experience in the new situation', (ibid: 101). Lado for instance, (1957) states "individuals tend to transfer the forms and meanings, and the distribution of forms and meanings of their native language and culture to the foreign language and culture" in speaking and understanding processes, (cited in Keshvarz, 2004: 5). Also, Brown (1994: 90) defines it as "carry over of previous performance or knowledge to subsequent learning".

The last use of transfer refers to a "characteristic of learners' performance". Therefore errors from different sources are referred to as 'transfer errors'. (Dulay, Burt and Krashen, 1982: 101)

There are some explanations for the occurrence of this linguistic phenomenon. According to the behaviourists', learners already have a well-established habit in their mother tongue, the new habits involve replacing these old habits by new ones, as a result the old habits interfere with the new and thus transfer occurs, (Mitchell and Myles, 2004: 30). Another explanation is provided by Newmark who states that the learner falls back on his L1 when he has not acquired FL sufficiently, (cited in Krashen, 1981: 65). And according to Monitor performance model, it is the result of the L1 as an utterance initiator; "first language competence may replace acquired second language", (Krashen, ibid: 7). Zoble (1983, 1984) sees transfer as a result to the obscurity of L2 rules. Two reasons are behind this obscurity: first, the L2 is typologically inconsistent in that it violates a universal implication pattern. Second, the rule itself is typologically variable, so that there are a large number of possibilities. Thus, in these cases falling back to the L1 occurs and L1 influence is seen, (cited in McLaughlin, 1987: 79). Thus, while this linguistic phenomenon is the result of performing speech before acquiring enough knowledge of L2 by the acquirer, in turn (low acquisition) occurs.

Keellerman (1979, 1983) considers transfer as a cognitive process in which decision is made on the bases of the learners perception of the similarities between both L1 and L2 structures and the markedness degree of the structures of the native language, (cited in McLaughlin, 1987: 79). Marked structures are irregular, infrequent and semantically unclear.

Thus transfer occurs when the difference between the two languages are seen to be great and when the structures involved are unmarked, McLaughlin (ibid).

2.8 INTERLANGUAGE

Generally, the concept of interlanguage has been highly influential in second language acquisition research since 1960s. It is coined and elaborated by Selinker (1972) to refer to the "interim grammars constructed by L2 learners on their way to the target language", (cited in McLaughlin, 1987: 60). It may be described as the language learner's knowledge of the target language. For Falk (1978: 36o), it is a systematic, incomplete, emerging competence which is formed when learners of one language acquire another language and is independent from both their native language system and that of the foreign language.

Other Researchers define interlanguage differently but all indicate the same sense. Dulay, Burt and Krashen (1982: 278) use this term with reference to the "speech or writing of second language learners in the second language". Mitchell and Myles (2004: 30) define it as a system which can be described at any point in time resulting from syntactic rules and a series of interlocking systems that characterize learner progression. (Ellis and Barkhuizen, 2005: 4) confirm that it is the "oral or written language produced by the learner" which serves as the primary data for the study of L2 acquisition.

Interlanguage is not the natural language; rather, it has certain characteristics. The first one is that it is *systematic,* i.e., it incorporates a system which is capable of producing novel utterances different from both the native and target language of the learner. The second is that it is reduced, in contrast with the native language whether in the number or complexity of rules or words and *systematically variable.* [2]

Systemacity indicates that they have the same route as the children's language, and variability means that so many forms are used by the learner within a short time as learners vary their performance, (Mitchell and Myles, 2004: 16).

The last one is *fossilization*[3], i.e., phonological, morphological and syntactic forms of production of the L2 learner do not conform to the target language, however, instructions and exposure to L2 is continuous.

Interlanguage refers to the second and foreign-language learners' language but not to the native speakers, (i.e., native speaker interlanguage). A number of different terms have been used to refer to this specified language system. Corder (1973:260) used the term *idiosyncratic dialect* to focus on the idea that the "learners language is unique to a particular individual and the grammar of this language is specified to that individual alone", (Keshaverz, 2004: 62). Also, Corder (1977) captured this insight through the term *transitional competence* by which he meant a "dynamic goal-oriented language system of increasing complexity" (cited in Johnson and Johnson, 1999: 175). Nemser (1971) uses the term *approximate system* which means learner speech at a given time is the patterned product of a linguistic system, [approximate language], distinct from [source language], and [target language] and internally structured, (cited in ibid: 176). Ellis (1985) terms it as *language–learner language*, whereas Spolsky (1989) calls it an *elegant variation for second language*. Finally, Ellis and Barkhuizen (2005) use the term *learner language*.

Although all these different terms emphasize a particular notion, they share the concept that this language variety constitutes a system in itself, no matter how elementary and inadequate it might be, by which some communicative needs of the learner are met, different from both the native language and the target one. It represents the idealized speaker's knowledge in a homogenous speech community of the L2 that consists of formulaic speech and creative speech, which linguistically serves as an output data. This output constitutes a certain type of code known as interlanguage talk, which is slower, less-complex, ungrammatical than native speaker's speech limited by the competence of the speaker, (Krashen, 1981: 128).

However, Johnson and Johnson, (1999: 176) point out that the concept of interlanguage led researchers to see knowledge of one language as being the norm against which other forms of language knowledge are measured. Sharwood Smith (1994) describes it as the L2 learner's systematic linguistic behaviour, in which the focus is on *behaviour*, that is, performance but not competenence. Likewise, Bley-Vorman (1983), states that most SLA research assumes that interlanguage should not be considered as an independent system as compared to native language.

2.9 FACTORS ON SECOND LANGUAGE ACQUISITION (SLA)

Learners vary in terms of certain behavioural qualities like (personality, learning style, aptitude, age, motivation), which are termed as individual learner factors, (Ellis, 1985: 99). Each of which affects the process of SLA and all are important factors, (Fillmore, 1979) (cited in Ellis, 1985: 99).

Central Concepts in Foreign Language Learning 15

There is still controversy on the problem as which language aspect is affected by these variables, rate or route. Research results show that it is the *rate* which is affected rather than the *route* of learning. Route of learning refers to the "transitional stages that L2 learners go through in acquiring properties of L2", (Ellis, 1985: 218) whereas rate refers to "the time it takes to pass through them", (Johnson and Johnson, 1999: 133).

Generally, both types of factors have social, cognitive and affective aspects. Social aspect is external, encompasses the relationship of the language learner with the L1 and L2 native speakers. Cognitive and affective aspects are internal to the learner.

2.9.1 General Factors

General factors are those variables that all learners have. They are not different in terms of their 'presence in a particular individuals' learning' but in terms of their 'extent' or 'the manner' in which they are realized, (Ellis, 1985: 100).

General factors include age, aptitude, motivation, cognitive style and personality.

1. Age is a variable which is mostly taken into consideration as it is easy to be measured. Age affects the route and rate of learning in different ways. It has been arrived to the fact that old learners like the young pass through the same stages when they learn a particular aspect of language. Bialy et al (1974) found out in his longitudinal study, that the acquisition of morphophonems in adults is similar to that in children. Cazden et al (1975) also support the claim that children, adolescent and adult learners undergo the same stages in processing linguistic data, (cited in Ellis 1985: 104). Concerning rate, it has been found out that older learners learn faster than younger ones. The research results of Snow and Hoefnagel-Hohle (1978), and Fatman (1975) point to this fact as their older subjects did better in syntax and morphology, (cited in Dulay, Burt and Krashen, 1982: 85).

Research findings indicate that children generally under ten who learn language in a natural environment 'attain-native like proficiency', whereas older learners progress initially but 'children usually surpass' them, Dulay, Burt and Krashen, (1982: 78). A number of explanations have been provided concerning the differences.

   a. The Critical Period Hypothesis: this theory claims that language is acquired naturally and without any effort or learning in a certain age which falls "within the first ten years of life", Penfield and Roberts (1959) (cited in Ellis, 1985: 107), because during this period the brain 'retains plasticity' but it declines 'with the onset of puberty', (McLaughlin, 1994: 91). Supporters to the critical hypothesis go further to the extent that they believe the effect of age is evident not only in pronunciation, but also in perception. It has been observed that the late learners are less proficient in discriminating the phonemic contrasts of the L2 than early learners, (ibid: 87). Studies like (Fledge, Yeni-Komshian and Liu: 1999) show that the early age exposure to a foreign accent would result in a native-like accent performance.

b. Cognitive Explanation: this theory is somewhat similar to the above one in terms of age .it can be clarified in terms of the different orientations of children and older learners towards language. Older learners are mentally matured and consider language as a formal system. They learn about language consciously. Children do not respond to form and they consider language only as a means to convey meaning. Thus, older learners respond to what language is but young learners respond more to what language does. (Halliday, 1973) cited in (Ellis, ibid: 108).

c. Affective Factors Explanation: affective means *emotion or feeling*. Affective factors mean emotional side of human behaviour. According to this theory, SLA is related to the stages of acculturation which is the ability to relate and respond easily to foreign language culture.

d. Krashen's monitor theory: according to Krashen's monitor model, children learn better than adults as they do not have a monitor and therefore not inhibited. According to 'affective filter hypothesis', children learn better than adults due to the strengthening of affective filter at about puberty. The filter is low in the case of children; therefore input is allowed to reach the LAD, while adults have higher filter because of the changes in adolescence. So, they are less developed in learning, (McLaughlin, 1994:28) and (Krashen, 1982:44).

2. Intelligence, traditionally intelligence is defined and measured according to logical and mathematical abilities. For Ellis (1985: 110), it is a hypothesized general factor which underlies the ability to master and use the whole range of academic skills. But for Mcdough (1981) it means "the *capacity* rather than *contents of mind*" (cited in Ellis, 1985:110).

There is no clear-cut conclusion whether this language faculty influences L1 or L2 acquisition or both. Oller and Perkins state that this intelligence affects SLA to the extent that "there exists *a global language proficiency factor* which accounts for the bulk of the reliable variance in a wide variety of language proficiency measures", (cited in Ellis, 1985: 110). But Ellis views that if this factor is not a major one in L1, hence it is of no such importance in L2.

The role of intelligence appears when it comes in classroom learning, but less in naturalistic environment as it affects the rate /success rather than the route of learning. Therefore, Spolsky's condition for intelligence is "the ability to perform well in standard intelligence tests correlates highly with school-related L2 learning" (1989: 102).

Gardener (1983) identifies seven types of intelligence: *linguistic, intelligence, logical-mathematical abilities, spatial intelligence, musical intelligence, bodily kinesthetic intelligence, interpersonal and intrapersonal intelligence* (cited in Brown, 1994:93).

It is mainly the first type which correlates with learning. However, musical intelligence predicts the easiness of perceiving and producing patterns of intonation of a language, whereas bodily-kinesthetic has a relation in terms of phonology. Interpersonal intelligence is of importance in 'communication processes' (ibid: 93).

3. Cognitive or Learning Style: it refers "to the manner in which people receive, conceptualize, organize and recall information which may interact with other factors of SLA, (Ellis, 1985: 144). It is the people's preferred modes of processing information, hence ways of learning.

Different dimensions of cognitive style have been recognized, such as field dependence-independence dichotomy, broad-narrow categorization, leveling-sharpening in memory. Field-independence is the concern of SLA field inquiry. Field-independence refers to "your ability to perceive a particular, relevant item or factor in a 'field' or distracting items", whereas field dependence style means the tendency to be 'dependent' on the total field so that the "parts embedded within the field are not easily perceived" (Brown, 1994: 105).

It is assumed that these two types of cognitive style are related to language learning in one way or another. Field-independents do some tasks more effectively than field dependents, whereas field-dependents acquire language more facilitative than independents as they gain such a success in formal classrooms. Thus, both styles are important in language learning in formal and informal learning situations.

4. Risk-taking: Risk taking is important in both natural and formal learning environment. Thus, Beebe (1983) states that:

> In the classroom, these ramifications might include a bad grade in the course, a fail on the exam, a reproach from the teacher, and a smirk from a classmate, punishment or embarrassment imposed by one. Outside the classroom, individuals learning a L2 face other negative consequences if they make mistakes. (Cited in Brown, 1994: 140) Also Brown states that learners must be able to 'gamble a bit' about language.

5. Aptitude: it is another intellectual ability to language learning. It is seen as "the language–related aspect of intelligence" (Cohen and Dornyei, 2002: 171). Different terms have been used to refer to aptitude such as 'a special ability, gift, knack, feel, or flair'.

The effect of aptitude can be measured according to proficiency levels achieved by different classroom learners. Claims about the effect of aptitude on learning are controversial. Neufel (1971: 17) views linguistic aptitude so important that "without it language learning...would be quite impossible." (cited in Dulay, 1982:111). For Krashen (1981) aptitude only affects one aspect of SLA, which is learning but not acquisition. Thus, "a person with a high aptitude will pick up L2 easily, whereas for another person with the same level of proficiency, learning can only be achieved by hard work and persistence" (Cohen and Dornyei, 2002: 171). Whereas Skehan (1986) finds out that such a factor does not determine whether someone is able to learn a language or not and it determines the rate of learning but not the route, (cited in Ellis, 1985:113 and (Cohen and Dornyei, 2002:171). Aptitude can be compensated by other learning factors, like high motivation, the use of affective language learning and learning strategies.

6. Personality: As far as personality is concerned, Johnson and Johnson (1999: 238) refer to it as traits of an individual which are independent from language and social context which is many-facets in nature. It is suggested that language learning takes different forms in accordance with personality. In other words, "varieties of personality are associated with different preferred modes of language learning." Language and language learning are related to personality to the extent that Guiora states, "language is not just a means of communication but a basic method of self-representation, incorporating, in a unique blend, intra and interpersonal parameters, cognitive and affective aspects of information processing, allowing a view of total person", (cited in Spolsky, 2002: 11). Anyway, personal traits that are related to language learning include Extroversion/Introversion, Self-Esteem, Anxiety, Self-Image, Outgoing Personality and Empathy, Inhibition, Attitudes and Motivation.

2.9.2 Personal Factors

Personal factors are highly idiosyncratic features of each individual, which involve nesting patterns, i.e., "the need for a secure and orderly home base before learning can effectively begin", (Ellis, 1985: 100), transition anxiety, i.e., "the stress generated by moving to a foreign place", (ibid., 100) as well as the desire to maintain a personal language learning agenda which affect SLA to a great extend. These factors are heterogeneous. They include Group Dynamics, Attitude to the Teacher and Course Material, Individual Learning Techniques.

2.10 THE ROLE OF SOCIAL CONTEXT IN LANGUAGE LEARNING

Language is a social mechanism. It is learned within the social context and it is not to be isolated from it. According to Roger's humanist psychological theory, if the context of learning is created in the proper way, learners will learn everything they need, (cited in Brown, 1994: 86).

Different models have been developed in order to explain the effect of social context on language learning. First, Spolsky's model of Conditions For Second Language Learning (1989) for L2 learning shows that social context affects language learning indirectly in two ways: it influences the learners' attitude towards the target language, its speakers and language learning situation which influence motivation indirectly; and it determines the 'social provision' of language learning situation and opportunities.

The social and political status of a language is significant in determining goals and opportunities to learn and attitudes towards the target language and its speakers. When a language is to be taught or preserve an immigrant language, there are a number of criteria to be met. First, the number of its speakers; the greater the numbers of the speakers of the language, the more learners wish to learn it, and vice versa. Second, is language distance; the closer the two languages, i.e., (L1 and L2), there would be more chance of mutual understanding and a shorter time it requires from the learner to learn it. The third criteria is seen very important in L2 learning which is the kind of language involved whether it is standard, classical language, dialects, pidgin or Creoles.

Schumann's acculturation model explains the significant of affective and social factors. Acculturation means "social and psychological integration with the target group", (Johnson and Johnson, 1999: 2). The relationship between acculturation and L2 acquisition is that L2 acquisition is "just one aspect of acculturation and the degree to which a learner acculturates to the language group will control the degree to which he acquires the second language", (cited in McLaughlin, 1994: 110). The psychological and social distance between the L1 and the target language determine the degree of acculturation and hence L2 acquisition. Thus "the closer they feel to the target language speech community the better learners will "acculturate and the more successful their second language will be", (Mitchell and Myles, 2004: 49).

Another model that clarifies the role of social context on language learning is that one summed up by Bell (1984) cited in Spolsky (1999: 133–135). Bell identifies two origins of language variation: linguistic and extralinguistic which have relations with sociological dimension. He develops this model on the basis of style axiom.

2.11 LEARNING STRATEGIES

Strategies are seen as "techniques used by L2 learners for remembering and organizing samples of the L2", (Johnson and Johnson, 1999: 195). More precisely, they are "specific methods of approaching a problem or a task, modes of operation for achieving a particular end and planned designs for controlling and manipulating certain information, (Brown, 1994: 104).

Strategies that are taken by the L2 learners result in different achievements as research results indicate. Kim (2005: 18) supports this view by stating that good language learners use different learning strategies more than less successful learners. Generally, L2 field study distinguishes between two major types of learner strategies; *language learning* and *language use* strategies. According to Cohen and Dornyei (2002: 178), learning strategies are "conscious and semi-conscious thoughts and behaviours used by learners with the explicit goal of improving their knowledge and understanding of a target language. Language use strategies, however, include 'retrieval, rehearsal, cover and communication strategies", (Brown: 1991) (cited in Cohen and Dornyei, 2002: 2–3).

Learning strategies incorporate with other related variables like 'underlying styles, personality variables, and demographic factors such as age, sex, ethnic differences'. They are related to input 'processing, storage and retrieval', i.e., taking in messages from the others, whereas language use strategies are related to the output, i.e., the way people productively express meaning and deliver message, Brown (1994: 114).

Moreover, a third type of strategy, self-motivation strategy, has been identified. It is used by learners to 'increase and protect' their motivation which has an empowering effect on them and makes language learners more 'committed and enthusiastic', even when the environment is informal and without instruction, (Cohen and Dornyei, 2002: 2–3). O'Malley and Chamot (1990) study a large number (about twenty four) strategies used by learners of English as L2. They categorized them into four types: cognitive, metacognitive, social and affective strategies: *Cognitive* strategies include language learning strategies and language use strategies, i.e., they include those processes that learners go through when they learn or use the target language. *Metacognitive strategies* refer to those processes that are consciously used by the learners to manage learning. While *social strategies* regulate emotions, motivations and attitudes. Finally, *affective* strategies encompass those chosen actions taken in to interact with the other learners or the other language users, (cited in Cohen and Dornyei, 2002: 180–181, and Cohen, 1996:4–5).

Back to Ellis's view of learning strategies and their categorization (1985: 164–188), he classifies the strategies that participate in the L2 learning into three classes: *learning, production* and *communication* strategies. Thus the learning strategy involved in acquiring formulaic speech is pattern memorization, a psychological strategy that occurs unconsciously. As for hypothesis formation both simplification and inferencing strategies are involved while creative speech requires a host of processes and strategies. According to his view the above processes and strategies are typically subconscious procedures, but they can also be conscious.

Accordingly, learning strategies have two sub-divisions; first, *simplification* which consists of "attempts by the learner to control the range of hypothesis he attempts to build at any single stage in his development by restricting hypothesis formation to those hypothesis which are relatively easy to form and will facilitate communication" (ibid., 171). Moreover, simplification includes *overgeneralization* (which is an important strategy in human learning). To generalize means to infer or derive a law, rule or conclusion, usually from the observation of particular instances. In second language learning it refers to the processes that occur while the learner acts within the target language; generalizing a particular rule or item in the second language beyond the restricted constraints, (Brown, 1994: 91) and *transfer*.[4] Second, *inferencing* is "the means by which the learner forms hypotheses by attending to input", (ibid: 172). It is used when the learner cannot derive rules by using overgeneralization or transfer, which also includes interlingual (which is the result of intake analysis) and extralingual (which is based on features of physical environment to make the L2 input comprehensible). Once the learner developed a hypothesis, he can test in different ways; receptively productively, metalingual an internationally.

Interlanguage variability is a reflection of rules differently autoamtized, formally and functionally. Thus automatization involves "both the practicing of L2 rules which enter interlanguage at the formal end of the stylistic continuum and the practicing of rules which are already in use in the 'vernacular' ". (Ellis, 1985:175)

Production strategies refer to the "utilization of linguistic knowledge in communication", (ibid: 303). Production is assumed to be similar to L1 production process, which consists according of three stages: a production plan, an articulatory programme, and a motor programme, (Clark and Clark, 1977) cited in (Ellis, 1985:76). Accordingly, these strategies are used by the speaker when he is unable to gain the original communication aims as it was arranged; therefore they are obliged to change the goal or to take other methods that can lead them to the same aim.

Production strategies, which are common for both first and L2 users, include planning strategies (i.e., planning of an utterance) encompasses semantic simplification, i.e., the reduction of propositional elements that are linguistically coded, and linguistic simplification, i.e., (the omission of form words and affixes) and correcting strategies or monitoring.

Communications strategies, which are exploited by both native speakers and L2 learners, are psycholinguistic plans used when learners face problems of language use. Communication strategies also involve two sub-categories: *reduction* strategies and *achievement* strategies. The former strategies can be formal (i.e., certain L2 rules are avoided) or functional where in certain speech acts or discourse functions are avoided, and achievement strategies that are activated when the learner decides to keep the original communication goal but compensates for insufficient means or makes the effort to retrieve the required items. So it subsumes compensatory and retrieval strategies, (Ellis, 1985:'180–182).

2.12 THE ROLE OF OUTPUT IN SLA

Researchers on L2 learning agree that output affects the increase of fluency, i.e., L2 utterance is to be produced by learners so as *to learn to use* their interlanguage rules confidently and routinely. Swain (1985, 1995) developed the Output Hypothesis in which she proposed other functions than practice of output which, in her view, relates to the interlanguage development. These functions are:

1. The noticing/triggering function: that is, the production of the target language makes learners aware of the L1 problems and 'gaps'.
2. Hypothesis testing function: this gives them the opportunity to 'experiment' with new structures and forms.
3. Metaliguistic function (reflective) role: it gives them the chance or opportunity to 'discuss and analyze' these difficulties. Mitchell and Myles (2004: 178).

According to Long and Porter (1985) 'interlanguage talk', which is a kind of group conversation between non-native speakers, is used to negotiate meaning, to affect the increase of communication, and to motivate the learners to learn. (McLaughlin, 1987: 50)

2.13 FORMAL INSTRUCTION

In formal language environments the focus is on conscious acquisition of rules of and forms; however "its role in the development of communicative skills appears to be quite limited". This is the conclusion that Dulay, Burt and Krashen (1982:19) seem to have arrived at. Ellis (1985: 223) tabulates the findings of twelve longitudinal and morpheme studies of Flex (1981), Schumann (1978), Fatman (1975), Lightbown et al (1980), etc, in classrooms where English is taught as a foreign language (EFL) and second language (ESL) to children and adults. The results indicate that formal instruction develops L2 knowledge which manifests itself in 'language use only where the learner attends to form', but it does not affect the natural route of SLA which is clear in communicative speech'. Route of learning refers to the transitional stages that L2 learners go through in acquiring properties of L2", (Ellis: 1985: 133).

Moreover, the empirical research results of other twelve studies on the effect of formal instructions on the rate/success of SLA which are summarized similarly by Ellis (1985: 228) indicate that formal instruction has a mixed effect: positive, ambiguous and no effect. But in general these results support the hypothesis that instruction aids the rate /success of SLA.

On the other hand, rate of learning refers to the "time it takes to pass through them", (Johnson and Johnson, 1999: 133). It is significant to mention that all of these studies examined 'relative utility' of instruction, i.e., they were concerned with the 'overall effects of instruction on L2 proficiency in relation to the effects of simple exposure to the L2 in natural setting'. None of the studies examined the absolute effects of formal instruction (except Ellis, 1984). Thus, it can be concluded here that formal instruction affects the rate of language acquisition but not on route.

2.13.1 Explanation of the Role of Formal Instruction

Three different positions have been put forward to give a clear explanation on learning. First, the non–interface position which is put forward by Krashen (1981). He distinguishes between acquisition and learning. Krashen sees that acquired knowledge compromises 'unconscious rules' which are called upon automatically by the language learner, whereas learnt knowledge contains metalingual knowledge which works only as a monitor on the produced speech.

These two kinds of knowledge are separate from each other; this means learning does not turn into acquisition, Krashen (1981) cited in Ellis (1985: 229). According to this position, comprehensible input can lead to acquisition rather than consciously learnt knowledge (or learning), Johnson and Johnson (1999: 174), as formal instruction "does not affect the developmental route because the learning it produces is powerless that can alter the sequence of development that occurs through acquisition", (Ellis, 1985: 232). However as formal instruction constitutes 'intake environment', it leads to development.

As for interface position which distinguishes acquisition and learning as two but not entirely separated knowledge as 'seepage' occurs from one knowledge to another. (ibid: 234). The weaker version of this position as Seliger (1979: 368) states, posits that the learned knowledge does not change into acquisition. However formal instruction facilitates acquisition by focusing learners' attention on "critical attributes of the real language concepts that must be induced" (cited in Ellis, 1985: 234), i.e., it helps the process of hypothesis testing in a better way. Stevick (1980) and Bailystok (1977, 1979, 1981) developed two different models. Though they, like Krashen, differentiate between the two kinds of knowledge, they suggest that learning turns into acquisition via practice. Sharwood Smith argues that formal instruction serves as a means by which conscious-raising can take place. (cited in Ellis, 1985: 235)

The variable position is the last one in this concern. It is different from the above positions as it recognizes different styles ranged from careful to the vernacular, the choice of the used style is a 'function of the amount of attention he is able to pay to his speech', (Tarone, 1983) cited in (ibid., 237). Each kind of knowledge is different in accordance with 'analicity' and 'automacity'.[5]

This position clarifies the role of formal instruction as it helps in internalizing these types of knowledge directly via 'intake environment' which is supplied by classroom, and indirectly by automizing learning through practice. This makes the formal learner to perform variety of tasks than the natural language learner.

NOTES

1. Code refers to the target language variety.
2. The causes behind variability may be linguistic, psycholinguistic, and/or sociolinguistic (Mitchell and Myles, 2004: 226).
3. Fossilization: is the phenomenon whereby linguistic items (particularly erroneous ones) become permanent in learners Interlanguage. (Johnson and Johnson, 1999: 135).
4. According to Brown (ibid.) all generalizing involves transfer, and all transfer involves generalizing.
5. Bailystok distinguishes between two continua 'analicity and automaticity'. For further clarification see Ellis, (1985: 238).

Chapter Three

Auxiliary Verbs in English

3.1 THE STRUCTURE OF THE ENGLISH VERB PHRASE

Traditionally, the sentence was defined in terms of the relationship between a subject and a predicate. In this sense, the subject is a noun phrase (henceforth, NP) and the predicate is a verb phrase. In consequence, a minimal sentence is a two-part hierarchal structure.

As far as the verb system in English is concerned, it has been analyzed differently according to two approaches. The first one is termed the *morphological approach*, (Quirk et al, 1985: 3–4). The verb phrase (henceforth, VP) incorporates two elements: the *main verb* and the *auxiliary system.* If there is only one verb in the VP, it is the main verb. But if there are more verbs other than the main verb, they are called auxiliary verbs. (henceforth, Auxiliary verbs). This analysis focuses on the internal verb system relation.

The second approach is the *syntactic approach* that is held by the transformationalists who divide the sentence into noun phrase and VP, which (more or less) involves the original division, subject and predicate. In this sense, the VP is composed of its components; verb (realized by VP) and its complementation (which is realized by the NP, AdjP, AdvP). This sort of analysis emphasizes the peripheral or external associations of the verb, (Quirk et al, 1985:16ff).

According to the syntactic approach, (which is broadly held by systemic grammar, dependency grammar, functional grammar, and case grammar), a sentence revolves around their verb as the element that determines 'what form the rest of the structure will take', (Navarro, 2002: 247).

Verbs in English are classified differently by grammarians. Quirk and Greenbaum (1990: 24) classify them into three major types: full or lexical verbs, primary verbs and modal auxiliary verbs, whereas Huddleston and

Pullum (2002: 74) classify them into two main types: the auxiliary verbs and the non-auxiliary or the lexical verbs. In this study the latter classification is taken as a model. Since lexical verbs are beyond the scope of this study, they are not explained here, what follows is a detailed discussion of English auxiliary verbs.

3.2 AUXILIARY VERBS

Auxiliary verbs (traditionally known as helping or supporting verbs) are a small set of words including primary auxiliaries like *be* and modal auxiliaries like *can* and *will*. Various definitions have been given for English auxiliary verbs. "Auxiliaries do not make up a verb phrase on their own but help to make up a verb phrase in combination with a main verb." (Leech and Jan Svartvic, 1994: 240)

According to Roberts (1956: 40) "auxiliaries are a set of words that pattern with verbs ... serve to mark verbs in a sentence". For Leech (2000: 240) "they are a small class of words which do not make a verb phrase by themselves except by the help of other verbs". In these senses, auxiliaries cannot stand by themselves, in the cases when they occur without the existence of the main verb, it must be implied earlier within the context[1].

Auxiliary verbs denote a closed class of verbs that are "characteristically used as markers of tense, aspect, mood, and voice. These categories are also commonly expressed by verb inflections (as primary tense in English for example). Auxiliaries tend to express the same kind of meaning as inflections, but are syntactically separate words", (Huddleston and Pullum, 2002: 102). They are a set of function words that are subordinate to the head verbs.

Auxiliary verbs in English are of two major types: *primary and the modals (or non-modal and modal verbs)*. Primary auxiliaries include *be, do* and *have*. They can function either as a lexical verb like:

- *I am a student.*
- *I did my job.*
- *I have a car.*

or as an auxiliary verb. In the latter case, they can generate all sorts of aspect (progressive, perfective) and passive constructions when combined with present or past participle:

- *I am studying.*
- *He has finished.*
- *It is done.*

The modals are a "group of independent words in English which express such concepts as permission, necessity or ability", (Tallerman, 1998: 66). Quirk et al (1985: 137) divide modal auxiliaries into five subgroups; Central, Marginal, Modal Idioms, Semi-Auxiliaries and Catenatives, as this division is based on distinctive formal features for each group.

Auxiliary verbs satisfy the morphosyntactic definition of verbs. They occur adjacent to the verb and carry at least some of the inflectional information (subject/object agreement and tense/aspect/ mood marking) that are normally associated with verbs. They do not embody the major conceptual relation, state, or activity expressed by the clause. They are often semantically 'empty, (for instance *do* in English: *He does go to school*), or they express auxiliary information such as tense, aspect, or mood, (Payne, 1997:84). Moreover, auxiliary verbs are a set of function words that are subordinate to the head verbs. *Have* and *be* are markers of tense and aspect, *do* is an empty or meaningless auxiliary that functions as an operator in do-support constructions. They can also be defined according to their ability to appear in some constructions such as inversion, code, emphasis, and negation. Unlike main verbs, auxiliary verbs group cannot stand-alone and always occur in combination of another verb. Thomson and Martinet (1986: 109) believe that "this set of verbs helps to form a tense or expression hence the name."

Auxiliary verbs can thus be considered an element that "in combination with a lexical verb, form a monoclausal verb phrase with some degree of (lexical) semantic bleaching that performs some more or less definable grammatical function". (Anderson, 2006: 5)

Syntactically and semantically, auxiliary verbs (primary or modals) are of great importance. They function as an operator, which is a "single word performs an operational function in relating a positive declarative structure to another major structure in the language", (Quirk et al, 1985: 80). In other words, they participate in forming interrogative and negative constructions:

- *She has been studying for a long time.* (Affirmative)
- *Has she been studying for along time?* (Interrogative)
- *She has not been studying for a long time.* (Negative)
- *He may come.* (Affirmative)
- *May he come?* (Interrogative)
- *He may not come.* (Negative)

As far as the operators are concerned, Quirk and Greenbaum (1990: 34) show the following characteristics:

1. The negative particle (not) is put directly after the operator.

2. In interrogative clauses, they initiate the sentence hence the subject follows.

3. They carry the nuclear stress to mark the positivity of a finite clause.

4. They function in a range of 'elliptical clauses' in which the predication is omitted, as in the following contexts:

a. So / Neither/ No +operator.

- Positive: *Sarah will be a doctor and so will Van.*
- Negative: *Dana will not be a teacher and neither will Ari.*
- Positive: *Tara arrived and so did her friends.*
- Negative: *Shena does not answer, nor does her brother.*

b. Operator + {too, either}.

- Positive: *I wrote her a letter and my sister too.*
- Negative: *I did not stay late and my friend did not either.*
- Predication fronting: *He said he would arrive late and late he was.*

c. Relativized predication: *He said he would break the promise which he did.*

Primary auxiliary verbs are meaningless alone; they acquire meaning only when they occur in the adjacency of another verb showing aspects and voice, and determining the tense of a phrase.

Accordingly, Whitehall (1956: 80) points out that the main function of this group of 'empty words' is to "limit the functions of the verb according to the attitudes and feelings of the speakers towards the happenings they may be reporting".

Thus, when there is a main verb in a sentence, it times the verb either past or present, but when it is clustered with auxiliary verbs, the particular manner in which a happening (is, was, or will be) may be recognized, whereas with the simple form verbs all this is implicit, unanalyzed and unstated. He calls this group of words *specialized modifiers* that precede the modified verb, together they build up verb-word groups that has a verb as its head, (ibid., 42).

Sometimes, ambiguity may originate in the absence of auxiliaries as stated by Roberts (1956:40) "in a way, auxiliary to verbs, what determiners to nouns". According to this view, these groups of words mark the verb in the sentence and detect the ambiguity in terms of the verb in sentence:

- *Army* demands *change.*

The reader cannot recognize to which part of speech does the word *demands* or *change* refer to, a noun or a verb. Therefore, he labels such a sentence as an ambiguous sentence. However, when an auxiliary is put before any of them, ambiguity will be disclosed as the auxiliary marks the verb:

- *Army demands may change.*
- *Army may demand change.*

As far as conversation is concerned, Thomson and Martinet (1986: 111) argue that auxiliary verbs are extremely important in conversation, "because in short answers, agreements; disagreements with remarks addition to remark, etc, we use the auxiliary instead of repeating the original verb".

3.3 FUNCTIONAL CRITERIA FOR THE AUXILIARY VERBS

The following criteria, applicable to operators, may help to define the auxiliary verbs as a functional class more precisely:
1. They function as operators to form:

a. Negative finite clauses: the negative particle is added directly without do support.

- *She is a teacher. ~ She is not a teacher.*

b. Inversion: in interrogative clauses whether WH-or YES/NO questions even in exclamatory sentences, the inversion of the subject and the auxiliary occurs.

- *She is nice. →Is she nice? (Open interrogative)*
- *She is studying. →What is she doing? (Closed interrogative)*
- *She tried hard. →How hard did she try! (Explanative)*

c. Reduced clauses or code: Palmer (1971: 74) states, "All the auxiliary verbs can stand for the whole of the verbal element for which they are or they were only the first word". Huddleston and Pullum (2002: 99) add that auxiliary verbs can function as operators in four types of reduced clauses known as code or stranding. In code constructions, "the VP of a clause is reduced, with the reminder of its semantic content being recoverable from the context."

3.4 SYNTACTIC PROPERTIES OF PRIMARY AUX. (BE, DO AND HAVE)

Unlike modals, the primary auxiliary verbs are different syntactically and semantically. They reflect tense, aspect and voice. They have inflectional and non-finite forms. Stagerberg (1965: 138) tags them to quasi-auxiliaries, which may precede the 'verb stem', the present participle and the past participle':

- *I do insist.*
- *They are working.*
- *We have finished.*

The following is a brief explanation for each of them:
   Be is unique among English verbs due to the following facts:
   a. It can function as a vital element in the aspectual and passive constructions; that is why grammarians call it the *aspectual* and *passive* auxiliary, for instance Kuiper and Allan (1996: 222) and Radford (1997:151).

- *They are building a new house. (Aspectual)*
- *The guests are being served. (Passive)*

   b. It is the only verb that has eight different forms (*be, is, am, are, was were, been, being*).
   c. It can function as a copular verb, which links non-verbal predicates (nouns, adjectives, and certain adverbials with their subjects) and serves as a carrier for tense and subject-verb agreement, (Celece-Murcia and Larsen Freeman, 1999: 53). Eckersley and Eckersley (1960:197) refer to *be* with the term *incomplete prediction*, as it requires some thing else (complement) to complete its meaning.

- *Lana is student. They are funny. Hezha is here.*

   d. It does not require *do-support* as a copular, except in commands:

- Do *be quiet.* which is more persuasive and implies more emotion than:
- *Be quiet.*

   However, the do–support is required in negative forms of imperatives:

- *Do not be awkward.* (Leech, 1975: 243).

Have can function as a main verb within the verb phrase under certain contextual circumstances. As an auxiliary verb, have is combined with the (-ed2) form of the verb (past or present) to form what is known as an aspectual and passive auxiliaries.

- I have answered your question. (present perfect)
- She had collected her papers. (past perfect)
- She will have worked hard. (future perfect)
- I would have worked. (perfect conditional)
- It have been done. (passive)

Moreover, according to Thomson and Martinet (1986: 122–123) the auxiliary have has other uses and as follows:
    a. Have +object +p.p: This construction is used to express neat senses:

- I had my house cleaned.

    b. Have+object+past participle: This construction can be used colloquially instead of a passive verb, when it was used for an accident or misfortune.

- He had his fruit stolen before he had a chance to pick it.
- He had his car damaged during the accident.

    c. Have+object+present participle: This construction is usually used with a future time.

- I will have you working in three days. (Because of my effort, you will be working in three days).

However, it can be used to indicate the past or the present respectively:

- He had them all laughing.
- He has them talk to each other.

When have occurs in its stative sense of possession, it is used as an operator (in BreE particularly):

- I have just seen him.

Eckersley and Eckersley (1997: 195) identify the general principle for have to be treated as an auxiliary as follows:
    When have conveys the meaning of 'possess' and this possession is a permanent thing:

- She has brown eyes.

and when speaking of one particular occasion:

- I have a headache.
- Have you a headache?

But, when this habit is habitual, have is not considered as an auxiliary:

- I often have a headache.
- Do you have a headache?

In informal use have got is used. It is similar in function as have as a 'state' verb and as an auxiliary (particularly preferable in negative and interrogatives). (Leech, 197: 242):

- You haven't got anything to persuade me. (Negative)
- How many books have you got in your bag? (Interrogative)

Conversely, when have functions in the dynamic sense, normally it takes the do-support, therefore the alternative 'have got' is not possible:

- He has milk for breakfast.
- He doesn't have milk for breakfast.

Do has the following forms *(do, does, did,)*, like a finite verb. It shows number, person and tense distinctions but it does not have non-finite forms itself. Thus, *do-support* applies to the use of do as an empty or dummy operator "where other constructions require an operator, but there is no semantic reason for any other to be present", (Quirk et al, 1985: 133). In addition, it has both the auxiliary and the main verb functions:

- *I did my job. (Main v.)*
- *Did you do your job? (Auxiliary verbs)*

Palmer (1971:74) points out that *do* is particularly important and special because it is the proform used where there is no auxiliary verb. These uses are as follows:

a. Negative: do-support is used to form negative present and past simple tenses where the verb is simple (present or past). Do carries tense and posits 'not' between the auxiliary and the main verb.

b. Interrogative: includes all types of questions and all constructions that involve subject–verb inversion instead of the default pre-verb position, such as tag-questions and reduced clauses, (Huddleston and Pullum, 2002: 94). In this sense, do serves as a carrier of tense and provides inversion that signals question, (Stagerberg, 1965: 138).

c. Emphatic: emphatic means "emphasis on an auxiliary realized by heavy stress."(Huddleston and Pullum, 2002: 98). It is used when we wish to add special emphasis on a speech that express doubt about the action referred to:

- *I did not see him.*
- *I did see him.*

Do-support is used for emphasizing positive and /or negative polarity in the clause where there were no any other auxiliary in the sentence.
  a. Emphatic polarity:

- *She 'did promise. I know.*

  b. Emphatic positives:

- *I did not know he was serious, but he was.*

  c. Emphatic in negation:

- *You misunderstood me, I 'did not tell her.*

Reduced clauses or code: in reduced clauses *do* functions as a *substitutive verb* whether there is a previous auxiliary or not, in order to avoid repetition, (Leech and Jan Svartvic, 1994: 479). Compare:

- *She likes fruit and her brother* likes *it, too.*
- *She likes fruit and her brother* does *too.*
- *I have sent it; my sister may* have *too.*
- *I have sent it; my sister may* have *done so.*

Thomson and Martinet (1986:479) group these uses of reduced clauses in:
  a. Short agreement and disagreement;

- *He smokes a lot. ~ Yes, he does /No he doesn't.*

  b. Additions:

- *He does not know the answer but I do.*
- *He likes concerts and so do I.*

c. Question tags: He teaches English, didn't he?
d. Short answers: *Did they attend? Yes, they did.*
e. Comparisons: *She knits faster than I do.*

f. When someone asks for approval or permission, *do* is used as an approval or encouraging affirmative answer: *Shall I sit here? Yes, do.* (Note: *Do* can be used alone without *Yes*).

g. However, Quirk et al (1985: 134) state that there is an exception where *do* precedes the verb *Be* as in imperatives:

- *Do be calm.*

It may be due to this fact that Radford (1997: 148) categorizes this verb under the modals [+M], i.e., it does not allow to be followed by a modal, no gerund forms:

- **Their doing speaking while studying.*

or infinitival:

- **She likes to do dance.*

Moreover, a double instance of *do* is ungrammatical. However, they share features of lexical in that they inflect for person and number.

3.5 MODAL AUXILIARIES OR THE MODALS

The Modals are sometimes called "verb markers as they signal that a verb is about to follow", (Stagerberg, 1956: 136). They precede the verb stem to give them special shades of previous meanings. Moreover, they are seen as stressless verbs that can occur immediately before a plain base and lack an-*s* part. Their purpose is to signalize non-actual situations, (Whitehall, 1956: 83). Modals are called so because of their contribution in modal meanings like possibility, obligation and volition, (Quirk et al, 1985: 120), or as "tenseless auxiliaries that take no subject agreement and no inf. to before the following verb", (Celece Murcia and Larsen Freeman, 1999:138). Modal auxiliaries are unlike the primary auxiliaries in several aspects. In other words, they are responsible for particular mood of the verb phrase and they cannot stand alone in the verb phrase to serve as a main verb.

3.6 SYNTACTIC FEATURES OF MODAL AUXILIARIES

Despite the general criteria for identifying the auxiliary verb group as a whole, modal auxiliaries have 'principal distinctive formal features', (Graver, 1986: 17) such as:
   1. Construction with the bare infinitive except for (ought to and used to).

- *He will be here next spring.*

   2. Modal Auxiliaries can only occur as operators in finite clauses but not in non-finites, *to may, * is /am/are + maying, *have/has/had + mayed.
   3. No inflection in the third person singular, no (–ing) form, no (-ed) participle: auxiliary verbs do not inflect for person, number and tense. Therefore such forms *wills, *mays. *cans are not possible forms. Due to this feature, they are sometimes called 'defective verbs' for example by Alexander (1988: 210). Huddleston and Pullum (2002:106) also state that the modals do not have secondary inflectional forms; hence they do not occur in constructions which require one. Thus and because of the lack of the two above features they do not appear in constructions like:

- **I'd like to can study.*
- But: *I'd like to be a teacher.*

   4. No concord with the subject or no subject-verb agreement: Modals fail to capture the subject-verb agreement because of their lack of inflectional feature:

- **He musts stay.*

   5. No appropriate time reference: when the modals occur in their present or past forms. They may denote past, present tenses, or even future time. Though there are historical past forms for them, they are not used to indicate past time as the case is with lexical verbs, Thomson and Martinet (1986: 111) state that past forms like *might, would, should and could* are just of past time in certain grammatical contexts like conditional clauses and indirect speech, but generally they occur in sentences to refer to now or future:

- *Could you help me?(* present time)

   6. No do-support use: do-support is not used with the modals in forming negative and interrogative constructions, as they function as operators themselves:

- *Do it will work?*
- *Will it work?*

7. No sequence of modals: in Standard English, two or more modals cannot chain. However, the modals are mutuality exclusive, in co-ordinations:

- *It may must call the police.*
- *They are having received my letter.*

In this concern, Alexander (1988: 210) states that in order to convey such a notion, we can use the alternate form:

- *It may be necessary to call the police.*

In spite of all these restrictions, modal auxiliaries in general are powerful in principal. They are necessary for forming negation, questions, for constructing contrasts of aspect and voice, (Finch, 2000: 130). Furthermore, modal verbs express certain speech acts like giving advice (ought to, should), threats (will) and giving orders (must, can) which add to the utterance 'force', (Quirk et al, 1985: 147).

3.7 CENTRAL MODAL AUXILIARIES

There are four paired sets of central modal auxiliaries with must: *can, could, may, might, shall, should, will, would,* and must. This group of the modals can only function only as auxiliary verbs. Huddleston and Pullum (2002: 106) point out that central modal auxiliaries have five distinctive properties: they have only primary forms (i.e.) they have no secondary inflection forms, they don't show any agreement with the subject, they don't show appropriate time reference (these are the properties of the modals in general as indicated in the previous section), they take bare inf. complement and they are required in remote conditionals.

- *I am canning to help you.* (only primary forms).
- *He shalls come.* (No agreement).
- *They must work.* (bare inf. complement)-(cf.): *They make us work.*
- *If you come tomorrow, [you could help with the flowers]*, (used in remote conditionals).
- *Could I answer?* (*could* does not mean past, though it is past in form).

However, it can be observed from the examples of (3.6) that the central modals have the other remained syntactic properties (6 and 7 above) but not mentioned by Huddleston and Pullum (2002). There is a group of verbs, which are intermediate between central auxiliaries, and main verbs. These verbs are of three types: marginal modals, modal idioms, semi-auxiliaries, (Quirk et al, 1985: 138).

3.8 MARGINAL MODAL AUXILIARIES

Marginal modal auxiliaries include such verbs like (dare, need, ought to, used to) that closely resemble the central modals, (Quirk et al, 1985:138). *Dare* and *need* can both occur as main verbs and as modals under limited conditions. They construct with the bare infinitive and do not have inflectional forms. Therefore, they exhibit abnormal time reference. As modals, their use is restricted to non-assertive contexts and those clauses that have semi-negative words like *hardly, only, scarcely*, etc. As main verbs, they have both uses, assertive and non-assertive, (Quirk and Greenbaum, 1990: 40) and (Quirk et al, 1985: 138).

- *Do you dare to call him a coward?* [Main v.]
- *Dare to call him a coward?* [Auxiliary verbs]
- *The rooms need tidiness, don't they?* [Main v.]
- *The rooms need tidiness, needn't they?* [Auxiliary verbs]

When *dare* functions as an auxiliary it has all the characteristics of them except two: first, it cannot be used in such constructions'. . . and so . . . I'.' 'Neither . . . I'. Second, "The adverbs of frequency come after it not before it", (Eckersley and Eckersley, 1960: 212). Similarly, Wouden (1996: 2–3) specifies the environments where *need* can occur that matches the auxiliary criteria. These include; negation, shifted negation, with semi-negative forms (*hardly scarcely*), in only clauses in the first argument of universal quantifiers, in comparative clauses, after superlatives, in before clauses, questions, with subjunctive force, in concessive clauses, and in protasis of conditionals.

When *need* and *dare* occur as main verbs, they inflect for the third person singular-s-ing participle,-ed participle:

- *He did not need to speak like that.*
- *He was so angry that no one dare approach him.*

Ought to is a verb of marginal-modal group that functions both as a main verb and as a modal auxiliary. Normally, it has the (to) inf., but in elliptical constructions the use of (to) is optional:

- *We ought to study hard.* [Auxiliary verbs]
- *Ought we to study hard?* [Auxiliary verbs]

- *Do you ought to study hard?* [Main v.] Less formal.
- *You oughtn't to smoke so much.* [Elliptical]
- *Ought I to give up smoking?*
- *Yes, I think you ought (to).*

When *ought to* is treated as a main verb its use with *do-support*, (which is a dialectical usage), is the 'least popular'. However, this is an indicator of all marginal status of this verb, like other marginal verbs shows tendency to pattern as main verbs,(Quirk et al ,1985: 140):

- *They did not ought to do such that sort of thing.* (Ibid, 1985: 140)

Used to is like *ought to*. It is followed by to-inf. and can function as an auxiliary (mainly in BreE) and a main verb. *Used to* indicates past habits or states, as it usually occurs only in the past tense:

- *Taxi wages used to cost 3000 I.D. (state)*
- *He used to go to school early. (habit)*

It does not have present forms (*uses to); thus, in present a repeated action is expressed by using simple present. It is for this reason that it is semantically not so much considered an auxiliary of tense and aspectexcept in form, (Quirk et al, 1985: 140):

- *He used to play football when he was young.*
- *Used to play when he was young? (aux)*
- *Did he use to play football when he was young?* (main v.)
- *Did he used to play football when he was young?* (is also used)

Used to is normally accompanied by *when*, a time adverbial which is described as a 'build-in' adverbial interpreted as 'once', and indicates an indefinite past time, (Leech, 1971: 49). As *used to* indicates past, it is not attached to such adverbials that determine the actual duration of a state or habit: **He used to smoke for ten years.*

Moreover its use with the perfect aspect (like other modal auxiliaries) never occurs. Used to is not equivalent to (be) used to [j: stu], which means (to be) accustomed to and may be followed by a gerund. For example: I am not used to getting up late. She is used to hard work. On the other hand, Payne (1997: 242) names this marginal auxiliary as an operator for expressing 'completive' aspect: *I used to walk to school*. Completive aspect expresses the completion of an event. Sometimes it is called 'phasal' aspect because they refer to different phases of the event described by the verb, (ibid, 1997: 242).

3.9 MODAL IDIOMS

The second set of verbs intermediate between auxiliaries and the main verbs are the modal idioms. They include; had better, would better, would rather/ sooner, be to, have got to. These are a group of multi-word verbs, which are a combination of an auxiliary and an inf. or an adverb. Generally, they share some features of main verbs and of auxiliaries. They are followed by an inf. (some times preceded by to) and do not have finite forms. Modal idioms do not occur as operators, normally their first word acts so, which is a feature of non-modal verbs and have aspectual and modal meanings, (Quirk and Greenbaum, 1990: 40).

- *They'd better stay here.*
- *You would rather not be in a hurry.*

3.10 SEMI-AUXILIARIES

Semi-Auxiliaries are a group of verb idioms or multi-word forms that all begin with the primary auxiliaries *be* or *have* and end with *to*. Like the above verbs, they share syntactic features of auxiliaries and of main verbs. Celece-Murcia and Larsen Freeman (1999: 134) argue that these verbs behave like main verbs more than modals, such as that, they occur in non-finite forms as (been going to, to be bound to). Moreover, Quirk et al (1985: 144) state that the occurrence of non-finite forms indicates that they can 'fill slots' in a modal verb paradigm, whereas other modals with the same meaning cannot occur. Semi-auxiliaries show subject-verb agreement and require to inf. precede the following verb, which in this feature depart from true modals. Moreover, they can chain with other auxiliaries as in:

- *I am going to be able to finish that work on Friday.* (though there are restrictions on this sort of combination)
- *The team is not going to win.*
- *Is the team going to win? [operator]*

But not:

- **The team doesn't be going to win.*
- *Does the team be going to win?*

Have to is the only verb in this group that begins with *have*, but it is involved partly because it has the full range of non-finite forms. It behaves differently from the rest, as it requires do-support just like main verbs Therefore, Gramely and Pätzold (2004: 128) term *have to* as a 'non-defective verb'. Semantically, *have to* is equal to *must* and is the alternative past form:

- *Do you have to stay here?*
- *I do not have to stay here any longer.*

There is a phonological evidence for the auxiliary nature of this verb group, which is the irregularity caused by the assimilation of infinitive marker to with the preceding element to form a single phonetic unit. Thus *have to* is really /hœf tə/ (has to is hasta, and had to is hadtə), have got to is gotta, supposed to is supposta, going to is gonna, etc. This sort of reduction is not applicable to other verbs, which are followed by inf., like (* love to~ lofta), (ibid, 2004: 128). In fact, they exhibit modal or aspectual meanings, i.e., semantically function as modals that each central modal has an equivalent counterpart (or more) of semi-auxiliaries, (Celece Murcia and Larsen Freeman, 1999: 159).

3.11 CATENATIVE-VERBS

Catenative word group includes verbs like 'appear to, come to, fail to, get to, happen to, manage to, seem to, tend to and turned out to' which are followed by inf. and other verbs that are followed by (-ing or–ed) participle. Generally, catenatives can be constructed with 'bare inf., to+ inf.,-ing participle,-ed participle). Gleason (1965) argues that the term catenative indicates "the fact that they form a chain of verbs", (cited in Saudi, 1984: 52), or "alludes to their ability to be concatenated in sequence of non-finite constructions." (Quirk et al, 1985: 147)

- *Our team seems to manage to keep on going beaten.*

This is the same feature of semi-auxiliary verbs and main verbs.

Catenatives are nearer to main verbs in their syntactic behaviour, as they have do-support in their interrogative and negative formation. Gramly and Pätzold (2004:128) define them as a "number of lexical verbs . . . semantically very similar to auxiliary verbs" for example, *want to* is equivalent to *will*. In addition, they share syntactic features of auxiliary verbs, i.e., independent of the subject in passive (which is a criterion of auxiliaries) and express meanings of modality and aspect.

3.12 ORDER OF AUXILIARY VERBS

Auxiliary verbs are employed in cluster of two or three or more according to specific syntactic rules in 'obligatory sequence' and form different types of tense, aspect, (Stagerberg, 1965: 138) as follows:

MODALS+PERFECTIVE+PROGRESSIVE+PASSIVE+MAIN VERB

The above sequencing underlies the inflectional relationships between each auxiliary and the verb that follows it. Each auxiliary determines the inflection form of the verb that follows it, (Kupeir and Allan, 1996: 234), whether this next verb is another auxiliary or a main verb. . This approach is called the 'geographical' or 'position' approach', (Navarro, 2002: 250). Accordingly, modals are followed by inf., perfectives are followed by (-ed) form, whereas progressive would have (-ing) form and passive auxiliaries entail an (ed2) verb forms.

Huddleston and Pullum (2002: 103) refer to this as 'core' use of auxiliaries and that "it is by virtue of this use that these verbs satisfy the 'general definition' of auxiliary verbs. Therefore, only core auxiliaries can be chained together in a sequence. However, other sorts of combinations of auxiliaries are not possible; *do* is not combined with any other auxiliary, and modals in general do not combine (criteria for modals no.7). Therefore, the top sequence to precede the main verb is four.

- *He could have been being finished studying.*

3.13 MOOD AND MODALITY

The difference between mood and modality is as that occurs between tense and time. Mood is a category of grammar whereas modality is of meaning. Therefore, it can be stated that mood is the "grammaticalization of modality within the verbal system", (Huddleston and Pullum, 2002: 172). Modality has been used in various senses. Generally, it may be defined as the manner in which the meaning of a clause is qualified to reflect the speaker's judgment of the likelihood of the proposition it expresses being true, (Quirk et al, 1985: 219).

Alternatively, Palmer (1990) notes that modality is concerned with our opinions and attitudes, (cited in Thompson, 2002: 3). Thus, modality "allows the speaker to introduce a personal interpretation of the non-factual and non-temporal of the event." (Lewis, 2002: 52). Hence, it does not mean the same as modal or modal auxiliaries, which are "one way for a speaker to introduce modality into what(s) he says." (ibid, 2002:3)

The area covered by modality is not so restricted and do not have typical features that to be referred to as such. It is rather a large area and finds expression in other areas of language, such as speaker's attitude to factuality or actualization of a situation, which is the main concern of modality. There is a semantic and syntactic difference between the unmodalised and modalised sentences:

- *He comes.* [unmodalised]
- *He may come.* [modalised]

In the former, the proposition is expressed without any qualification. In the latter, there is an additional qualification from the speaker to the truth of the proposition. Modality might be 'subjective', i.e.; it conveys the attitude of the speaker or other persons or 'objective':

- *You must leave the room.* [subjective]
- *Scientists think there is no life on other planets.* [subjective]
- *If x is a prime number between 90 and 100, it must be 97(it means x which is 97.* [objective]

Worth noting, Lewis (2002: 102) identifies 'one important way' for the distinction of the verb phrase containing a modal auxiliary and those, which do not. "A verb phrase which does not contain a modal auxiliary is "about" the subject of the sentence" whereas "Statements or questions which contain a modal auxiliary are about two people-the subject, and the speaker (in statements) or listener (in questions)".

Both necessity and possibility represent another area that modality covers. Huddleston and Pullum (2002: 173) state that possibility indicates "an open attitude to the truth of the proposition", (ibid, 2002: 102):

- *He may have left the room.* [the actualization of the situation is far]

Moreover, modality can be expressed via various linguistic expressions, such as *lexical modals*, which express the same kind of meanings as the modals but they are not of the same syntactic category. Lexical modals include AdjPs like: *possible, necessary, likely, probable, bound, supposed;* AdvPs and PPs like: *perhaps, possibly, necessarily, probably, certainly, surely;* number of verbs (VPs) like: *insist, permit, and require;* and NPs like: *possibility, necessity, permission. Past tense* is used to express modal remoteness. However, past perfect may be used to convey the same meaning. *Other verb inflections* in non-finite clauses, the infinitival is used with a modal sense. *Clause type*: the two finite clause types: interrogatives and imperatives are associated with modality. Imperatives are characteristically used as directives where the speaker typically wants the actualization of some future situation. And the interrogatives are used to express questions to which the speaker does not know the answer. *Subordination*: the declarative clause type is usually associated with factual statements.

However, such a realistic expression is often changed to a modalised (like subordinates form) it covey a different meaning. For example, *I know Sara is here* is different from *I suppose Sara is here*. One of the most important types of these types of clauses is conditional clauses that require an auxiliary in the matrix that has a modal use of the past in both clauses (subordinate and the matrix). *Parenthetical*: it includes such lexical modals like; *think,* seem . . . etc.

3.14 THE TRI-DIMENSIONALITY OF THE MODALS

The group of modal auxiliary verb's meaning and usage are different in terms of three dimensions namely: strength, kind and degree of modality. The first dimension deals with the "strength of commitment (prototypically the speaker's commitment) to the factuality or actualization of the situation, (Huddleston and Pullum, 2002: 175). Here two modal concepts are identified: *necessity* that involves a strong commitment and *possibility, which* includes a weak modal meaning. Moreover, the third type is seen on the scale that is closer to the strong end, it is labeled as medium modality. There is a logical relationship between necessity and possibility according to the initial remarks.

When dealing the strength of modality it is worth noting to point to the distinction between *semantic* and *pragmatic strength*, in the sentences like:

- *You must leave the room now.*
- *You must have lunch with me.*

Although both the above sentences are modalised with (must), they indicate different meanings according to the contextual use. The first sentence is an *instruction to leave* that indicates strong modality, whereas the second indicates an offer (conveys a relatively less strong modal meaning) which is labeled as 'pragmatic weakening. Similarly in:

- *You can park here.*

The former (you can park here) can be interpreted as permission (a police officer may permit a driver to park), while the latter's situation is different. This sentence, (you can do it alone), is used by a teacher when giving homework to his students and order (or instruct) them to do it without assist of anyone else. Therefore, it does not indicate permission. This is labeled as 'pragmatic strengthening', (Huddleston and Pullum, 2002: 177).

As far as kinds of modality, three major[2] types are identified, *epistemic, denotic* and *dynamic* modalities. Epistemic modality concerns with the speaker's attitude to the factuality of past or present time situations whereas denotic modality deals with "speaker's attitude to the actualization of future situations", (ibid, 2002: 178). It includes such matters as imposing, obligation and prohibition, permission, etc. The key terms are *permission and obligation*. The former is propositional, i.e., it has to do with beliefs and knowledge about logically possible or logically necessary situations, whereas the latter is event[3] oriented, i.e., it has to do with potential actions.

Dynamic modality deals with "properties and dispositions of persons . . . etc, referred to in the clause by the subject noun phrase" such as, *He can beat everyone here,* (ibid: 2002, 178).

According to Quirk et al (1985) and Quirk and Greenbaum (1990), two groups of constraining factors affect in the meaning of the modals; the first group includes a sort of intrinsic human control like , permission, obligation and volition. The second group does not involve human control of events, but rather involves human judgment over the events, such as possibility, necessity and prediction. On these bases, the groups of modals, which express the first kinds of meaning, are termed as *intrinsic* and those used to express the second group of meanings are labeled with *extrinsic* modal verbs.

Modal meanings also vary in terms of the third dimension, the degree; the "extent to which there is a clearly identifiable and separable element of modal meaning."(Huddleston and Pullum, 2002: 179). Thus, degree is quite different from the strength. The epistemic modals have two degrees, *High* and *Low*. The distinction can be well seen between modalised and unmodalised sentences like:

- *I recognize her.*
- *I may recognize her.*

The two sentences suggest two different concepts; the latter has a large degree of modality.

Sometimes modal auxiliaries may occur at the adjacency of a number of adverbs with the same degree to express, modal harmony, a single feature of modal meaning:

- *They must surely be invited to the party.*

Conversely, when a modal is combined with an adverb with a different degree, modal harmony is not achieved, for instance *may surely.

3.15 THE SEMANTIC ASPECT OF AUXILIARY VERBS

The primary auxiliaries are all empty operators as they indicated in the previous section. Verb to *be* functions as an empty operator and a linking element that carries tense and subject-verb agreement. Similarly, *do* and *have* are operators, which are of no interest semantically. *Do* is just a 'semantically empty syntactic component' in sentence processes as negation and interrogation, *be* participates in aspect and voice, whereas *have* only has a share in aspect, (Quirk et al, 1985: 120), whereas each modal verb has its specified meaning(s).

3.15.1 The Semantic Aspect of the Modals

Many modal lexis like *must* can be used to express all of the kinds of modal meanings:

- *It must be raining.* [after observing people coming inside with wet umbrella: epistemic modality]
- *Visitors must leave by 6:00 p.m.* [hospital regulation: denotic modality]
- I *must* sneeze. [given the current state of ones nose: dynamic]

Therefore, Palmer (1979) describes modals as 'messy,' However, he suggests, "(This) must not to be taken to imply that we cannot look for a fairly generalized common meaning or a set of closely related meanings for each modal", (cited in Lewis, 2002: 99). The main auxiliary types of epistemic and denotic necessity[4] and possibility are *must, need, may and can* respectively. According to (Huddleston and Pullum, 2002: 178)'s definition that epistemic modality expresses an attitude of the speaker at the present or past time towards a situation. In this concern, *may* and *must* are often used subjectively but the objective use is not excluded either:

- *She must be right.* [subjective]
- *Children at the age of six must attend school in this country.* [objective]

The modal *must* for possibility is used only in affirmative constructions; therefore, *can* is alternative in interrogative constructions and its negative counterpart *can't* in negative ones:

- *She must be the one you mean.*
- *Can she be the one you mean?*
- *She can't be the one you mean.*

However, when *must* is being used in the necessity sense, its alternative for negative and interrogative would be *needn't* and *need* respectively:

- *They must arrange the house.*
- *They needn't arrange the house.*
- *Need they behave like that?*

Similarly, *'may'* has both subjective and objective[5] uses:

- *He may be still in bed.* (subjective epistemic)
- *She may have missed the bus.* (epistemic objective)

When *must* is used in its necessity meaning, it can be interpreted as that the speaker reached at a conclusion from a known thing, (Leech, 1971:72). In this sense, it is similar in meaning with *may* for possibility. Normally, subjective use of these modals often involves pragmatic weakening whereas the objective one involves *strict semantic* necessity, which was explained earlier. In spite of that, the subjective/objective distinction is not always clearly maintained:

- *Senator Withers may have misled parliament*

The above sentence is said by the Australian Prime Minister of a politician who was accused for deceiving the parliament. It can be interpreted subjectively as; the parliament would be committing himself to this possibility, or objectively; the prime minister be admitting that others had made this accusation. [The example is from Huddleston (1984)] cited in (Gramley and Pätzold, 2004: 126). Denotic necessity (strong obligation) in affirmative contexts and denotic possibility (permission) are mainly expressed by the modals *must* and *may* respectively. The denotic *must* is subjective. Being used in questions, the authority and power shifts away from the speaker to the hearer:

- Must I tidy my room? (i.e., are these your orders?)

Cling to this subjective principle, in certain situations *must* is used with the first person subject in statements to convey the notion of 'self-compulsion', i.e., the speaker exerts power over himself, perhaps through a 'sense of duty, self discipline, or a sense of expediency', (Leech, 1971: 72):

- *I must finish my homework tonight.*

The objective form (of must) is *have to,* "which invokes an outside obligation which takes the onus of the speaker", (Gramley and Pätzold, 2004:126).

As far as permission, *can* is used in informal situations as a less 'polite' and less 'correct' than *may,* which is felt to be the very respectable alternative form:

- *You must do your homework.*
- *You may sit here.* (formal)
- *You can sit here.* (informal)

In terms of time, denotic modality indicates the future (especially with event verbs like, go, come, etc,). It can refer to past or present time with general 'requirements, conditions, options . . . etc:

- *They must have finished their work by 12.00 o'clock today.*

Should does not mean the same as (shall +past form) as some books of grammar indicate, for instance Show (1986: 107). In the most frequent uses as it is not derived from *shall*, it can be used epestimically and denotically. Epestimically its interpretation is a matter of *what I expect will happen* whereas denotically it can be interpreted as *what is expected of someone to do*. When it is used epestimically, it is usually subjective. It may also involve inference:

- *If this is not your handwriting, I should have failed to make the right guess.*

In the denotic sense *should* is also usually subjective. It indicates factuality (what is right for the speaker). *Should* is weaker than *must* as it permits 'not actualization'. Therefore, it is used with both past and present occasions in non-actualized situations. *Should* may appear in constructions with a rather different meaning from its *basic modal meaning* as it conveys a low-degree of modality in mandative, adversative, purposive, emotive and conditional constructions.

Ought to is the same as *must* in expressing the same epistemic and denotic meanings (but it implies rather lack of full confidence), (Quirk and Greenbaum, 1990: 63) and (Leech, 1971: 94).

- *The lights of her room are on, she must be in.* (and she is)
- *The lights of her room are on; she ought to be in.* (but not sure)

In conveying extra meanings, like tentativeness, *ought to* and *should* can be used alternatively:

- *You ought to be /should be at college in this age.*

Will is a modal auxiliary of lower degree of modality that can be used to convey the meaning of epistemic modality in epistemic, futurity and conditional constructions as follows:

- *They will have arrived by now.* (epistemic)
- *If I have time, I will help you.* (Conditional)
- *She will finish writing her thesis soon.* (Futurity)

Epistemic *will* is like *must* in terms of semantic strength, so it can be replaced by *must* in central epistemic sense. *Will* does not match with the other modals, as it cannot form modal harmony because they all have different meaning from *will*. Concerning dynamic meaning of *will*, it covers subjective referent dispositions and properties:
a. Volition

- *I will be there in time.*

b. Propensity

- *Sugar will milt down in water.*

c. It is used with the first person to indicate determination and resolution

- *We will pay the bills immediately.*

However, Huddleston and Pullum (2002: 194) indicate that the denotic of *will* is a matter of 'implicature'. Thus if the speaker (I) predicts the agent action of the hearer in contexts where I authorize, then I will be understood as tacitly invoking that authority:

- *You will see him and tell him what I told you.*

Shall has denotic and non-denotic, i.e., epistemic meanings. Denotically *shall* is seen to have these meanings when it is being used with the second or the third person:
a. Constitute/regulative use:

- *The parliament shall meet at least three times a month.*

b. Speakers guarantee:

- *He shall be rewarded if he is patient.*

c. Direction questions:

- *Shall I bring you a cup if tea? Yes, please do.*

When *shall* is used with the first person subject, it substitutes *will* in certain uses, like futurity, conditional and volition. However, in central epistemic meaning it does not replace it, as this usage does not cover first person subjects.

Three types of volition with *shall* have been identified, but unlike *will* as the volition in this case stems from the speaker as stated above:

a. Weak volition, i.e., willingness

- *You shall stay with us as long as you like*

b. Strong volition, i.e., insistence

- *No one shall stop me to go there*

c. Intermediate volition, i.e., intention

- *I shall write you soon*

The modal idiom *had better* and the marginal auxiliary *dare* have more restricted uses than the auxiliaries being discussed up to now. Each expresses only one kind of modal meaning. *Had better* conveys denotic meaning and generally co-occurs with subjective referents (which conveys strong recommendation but not compulsion) in present time, and the negation is internal.

- *He'd better not behave like that.* (I warn him . . .)

Huddleston and Pullum (2002: 196) state that *Had better* is semantically a strong modal as it does not imply 'non-actualization', but pragmatically a weaker one:

- *I/you had better wait.* (but suppose she wouldn't do)

Dare conveys only dynamic meanings, as an auxiliary means 'has the courage'. From its meaning, *dare* expresses speakers' deposition in declarative main clauses. Dare is normally negative and the negative is external; therefore, it is a weak modal:

- *I daren't tell him the truth.* (I don't have the courage to tell him . . .)

3.15.2 The Meaning of Semi-Auxiliaries

In order to identify the meanings conveyed by the semi-auxiliary verb group, Westney (1995) has proposed certain semantic criteria, (cited in Blanco, 2002: 6):
   a. Lack of subject restriction

- *The girl/the bus is supposed to be here at ten.*

   b. Voice–neutrality: sentences with semi-auxiliaries can be passivized without any change of meaning that it conveys:

- *Many people are supposed to receive the president.*
- *The president is supposed to be received by many people.*

   c. Idiomatic status ,i.e., "the lexical item taking part in their structure expresses a meaning which is different from the one it has in other contexts" (ibid, 2002: 6). For instance, be supposed to is used to convey the meaning of 'alleged' or 'believed, (Huddleston and Pullum, 2002: 208).
   d. Modal meaning: all the semi-auxiliaries express modal meanings, like probability, obligation, necessity . . . .

3.16 TENSE, TIME AND THE MODALS

Modal auxiliaries essentially refer to the moment of speaking (or the future) when used with the inf. form of the main verb. The use of the past forms *could, would, might, should* suggest a more tentative attitude of the speaker. In requests, it represents politeness, (Graver: 1986: 18). They do not refer to past time:

- *Could you pass the salt, please?*
- *Would you do me a favor?*

However, this particular use of this set of modals is consistent with their appearance of two forms of conditional sentences, (Graver: 1986: 18).

- *If you went out, you would get wet.* (unreal)

- *If I had known how it worked, I could have told him.* (contra factual conditions)

Therefore, in order to express past time reference of the modals there are certain methods:

- *It could/might be true now.*
- *It could/might have been true, then.*

Thus, the epistemic modality can be referred to the past by means of the perfective *have* and the *past participial* form of the main verb. This use has a contra factual effect, (Gramley and Pätzold, 2002: 125).

- *They might have done it.* (but they didn't)

In the denotic sense, there are substitutive forms such as the use of semi-auxiliaries. Therefore, *could* is not the past form of *can, might* for *may*, etc. Thus, from these four past forms: *could, would, might, should*, only the first two modals are used to refer to the past time when followed by inf., *Might* also can be used (but rarely). This can be done within a limited range of meanings. *Could* is used like *can* in all denotic and dynamic uses except when the matter is actualization, where *was able* is used instead. *Would* is used with dynamic modality (volition, propensity) and futurity. Whereas the use of *might* is restricted to literary style, (Huddleston and Pullum, 2002: 197), *should* is not used to indicate past meaning.

Moreover, the use of these four modals is 'automatic' in reported speech, (Graver, 1986: 19) and (Quirk, 1990: 301), (Thomson and Martinet, 1986: 270), i.e., they are not back shifted. Semantically, back-shift can be explained as "the time of the original utterance in the direct speech is now, becomes then for reported speech", (Leech, 1971: 100).

- *I said he (could, would, might, should) tell me.*
- Whereas other forms like *ought to, must* are left without back shifting, as they do not have past forms:
- *'He (can, will, may, should) tell me.*
- *I said he (could, would, might, should) tell me.*
- *'He (must not, ought not to) tell any one.*
- *I said he (mustn't, ought not to) tell any one.*

3.17 TWO DIFFERENT TREATMENTS OF MODAL MEANINGS

3.17.1 The Pedagogical Proposal

Celece-Murcia and Larsen Freeman (1999: 141–147) serve a pedagogical frame to deal with the meanings of the modals. Their first impression about the meanings of the modals is that they form a semantic opposition with ordinary tensed verb forms; the speakers of English use the modals they interject their perspectives and a proposition more subjectively than when only using simple tenses (past or present).

Several reasons are set behind the use of the modals, such as giving a proposition a degree of probability, expressing the attitude of ones self and variety of social functions (including politeness indirectness when making requests and giving advice or granting permission).

Two functions of modals have been distinguished: logical probability and social interactions, which are parallel to the epistemic and denotic functions.

- *You may leave the room* (social function)
- *It may rain tomorrow* (logical probability)

When the modals are used for social interaction, the user must take into account two things; first, the relevant features of the social situation, which are in this respect his/her status or authority upon the interlocutor. Second, the formality and informality of the situation, which enable him/her choose the suitable modal auxiliary in any interaction.

Another distinction between meaning and use of the modals is made. Logical probability is considered as meaning and the social function is the use. The logical meaning of this verb group deals with the speaker making an inference or prediction. The meanings conveyed by the modals are set in a hierarchy. They increase in the degree of certainty with regard to the speakers' inference from low to high certainty (could-might-may-should-will-must).

Use is the second function of the binary functions of the modals. Both present and past forms of the modals are used to express certain social functions like making requests. Requests are two folds; requests of general nature and specific requests for permission:

- May/might/can/could I have a word with you?

Another use of the modals is their systematic use in giving advice. The systematicity is observed when the modals can be ordered according to the degree of authority of the speaker or urgency of the advice: Advice can also be expressed negatively, which also have a systematic order from the stronger to the weaker advice.

The meaning of the modals is not confined to the above given ones, but goes further to involve potential realization, which includes ability, potentiality with *can and* desire by using *would like*:

- *He can sing well. (ability)*
- *This lorry can carry be loaded by over than 10 tons. (ability)*
- *He would like to travel away.* (desire)

Finally, offer or invitation with *would you like* which takes a question form:

- *Would you like this food?*

This proposition covers the semantic and pragmatic aspects of the modal verbs which helps better understanding of English modals by English second language (, henceforth, ESL) and English foreign language (henceforth, EFL) learners.

3.17.2 The Semantic Proposal

One of the semantic analyses for the explanation of the semantic aspect of modal auxiliary verbs is that by Leech (1969: 2002). Leech takes on the underlying logical meanings and the underlying relationships between the modals as the main concern of this analysis, as they are the 'bone structure' of the usage of the modals.

This analysis includes the discussion of the logical meanings of only six modals; can, *may, have to, must, will and shall,* which are set with their paraphrased meanings as in the dictionary. In order to avoid ambiguity of resemblance and contrast, the modal uses are summarized within six boxes; each box incorporates two modals identical in meaning; for instance *may* and *can* share the same box for possibility. The meanings encoded by these boxes seem to be covered by three major concepts; authority, contingency and volition.

Authority underlies *permission and obligation,* contingency involves *possibility and necessity* and volition includes *willingness and insistence* respectively. Meanings which are underlined the same concept are found to be related logically by a system termed as 'inversion system' or 'inverseness', that is "if one term is substituted for the other and the position of the negative is changed, the utterance undergoes no change of meaning" (Leech, 1971: 47). Thus, permission is the inverse of obligation, possibility for necessity. For instance,

- *Some students may stay outs after eleven o'clock = Not all students have to be in by eleven o'clock.*

The description of the semantic contrasts of the modal notions is provided by using seven types of systems: causation, actuality, constraint, authority, volition, ability, and probability which constitute the components of the semantic structure of the modals; hence, the componential approach that Leech adopts for this analysis.

To sum up, in this chapter the basic structure of English VP has been discussed for shedding light on the auxiliary verbs of the language. Complex VP is a combination of an auxiliary verb (or more) and a main verb. Auxiliary verbs have been classified into two major types: primary and modal auxiliaries. Primary auxiliaries include *be, do and have*, whereas the modals have been sub-classified into five subgroups which encompass *central, marginal, modal-idioms and catenatives*. Each group covers a number of verbs.

Auxiliaries are unlike main verbs; there are certain criteria by which one can distinguish auxiliary verb group from other verbs. Moreover, the modals can be distinguished from other kinds of auxiliaries via certain distinctive features that applicable to them. Furthermore, each auxiliary verb group has certain syntactic function (s) in the grammar of the language, like showing aspect, voice and mood. Moreover, even each modal auxiliary has certain semantic function (s) that contributes in consolidating the meaning of the sentence in general.

3.18 AUXILIARIES IN KURDISH

The verbal system is one of the most difficult aspects of the Kurdish language that has been the focal of study by Kurd and foreign linguists and grammarians. Understanding this system clears the path towards understanding the whole syntactic structure of the language since they 'constitute the entire utterance' (McCarus, 1958: 52). For example, the verb [dabim] (I will be) shows subject, object, person, tense, aspect, voice, mood, number and case marking.

There is abundant literature on the taxonomy of Kurdish verbs in terms of their indeclinable particles and other lexical items in their formation starting from Wahbi (1929: 28) up to now. Nonetheless, they all fall into two camps: traditional and structural. According to the traditional view, verbs are of three types; simple, complex and compound, whereas the structural view like Ma'ruf (1989: 40ff), Muhammad (2001: 25) refute the existence of simple verb forms in Kurdish entirely and make a distinction between two major types; complex and compound verbs.

3.19 AUXILIARY VERBS IN KURDISH: A TRADITIONAL PERSPECTIVE

[bûn] and (to be) and [habûn] (to become) are two intransitive verbs,(Baban, 1997: 4), which share the same root [b]. They are the most common Kurdish verbs known as auxiliary verbs traditionally that can function as main verbs, too. [habûn] is called a transitive verb by some grammarians like Ali Amin (1986: 243). Moreover, [bûn] has been named differently by different grammarians. McCarus (1958: 55) refers to it as the copula in such a sentence like:

- *[ganj bûm]* I was young

Wahbi (1929: 14), Alani (1984: 15) and Bomba (2000: 55–56) give *[bûn]* the statues of defective verbs that can not form a predicate by itself like any normal verb to convey the meaning or show a state of the subject, unless when it occurs with another verb, noun or derivative adjective. Therefore, [bun] cannot function as a main verb. Yet Alani (1984:15) does not deny that this verb can occur as a full verb, either. Ali Amin (1986: 241) includes it under the heading of weak verbs when he distinguishes between strong and weak verbs.

But in fact [bûn] is neither a defective nor a weak verb, (Fakhri, 1995: 38) and (Musa, 2000: 4). It has the full range of forms, (Alani, 1985: 15). Despite the past and present, it can be used to indicate continuous and future times.

Similarly, [habûn] is known as a defective verb among such grammarians and researchers like Soane (1913: 80) and Mackenzie (1961: 190), but they do not refer to the reason of this defectiveness directly. It can be clarified by the fact that [habûn] cannot be inflected to form imperative mood, nor forms like [haba, habin], whereas their alternatives are [biba, bibin] are more plausible. Moreover it can not be used with other verbs to form past perfect *[xwārd habû] or pluperfect *[xwārd habû bû], (ibid, 2000: 73). So, it does not have the full range of forms.

Recently, Musa (2000: 18) considers these two verbs as one verbal element [ha (bûn)], consisting of the possessive morpheme [ha], the verb root [b] and the past morpheme [û] and the infinitive marker [-n].

As an auxiliary, [bûn] contributes in the formation of variety of tenses, aspects and moods. [ha-bûn] as an auxiliary is like [bûn] semantically. It is the combination of [ha], a meaningless particle which is not used in writing alone, and [bûn]. Their status as an auxiliary has been recognised long ago.

Grammarians have different views for the auxiliary nature of these verbs and they adopt different views in terms of their forms. Soane (1913: 37–38) for instance, treats these two auxiliary verbs side by side and as 'identical in form and use' and states that they exist in sentences in two forms: first, as an independent form [bûn] and [habûn]. Second, as dependent affixial forms like [-m,-in,-n-,-n,-a] that occupy the 'ultimate position of a sentence'. This erroneous concept has remained dominant up to the present. As for Mackenzie (1961: 187), these two auxiliaries occur as enclitic forms attached to the *final ends of verbs* to form compound verbs as in:

- *[min dnyā nadit a]* (I have not seen the world).

Similarly, Hawramani (198: 129) and Amin (1986: 229) show similar views like Soane, i.e., [bûn] and [habûn] occur as final affixial verbal particles in the nominal groups rather than verbal ones. They may be attached to the noun end as in:

- *[aw mirov a]* (He is a human being), or an adjectives:
- *[aw źīr a]* (He is wise).

Even Fakhri (1995: 36) who refutes the notion of the defectiveness of [bûn] and refuses its existence as a weak verb, she holds the same view that in the present [bûn] has the contracted form [-a], which is attached to the end of a nominal element. So, her definition for the auxiliaries in this position is that:
They are those verbs which are introduced to nominal sentences which lack a verb to complete them. Auxiliary verbs does not indicate an action, but they are added to such incomplete sentences to make them a sentence, that is why they are called auxiliary verbs" (ibid, 1995: 35). Furthermore, Thackston (2006:25) is among the traditionalists as he repeats the same notion of the existence of enclitic forms of the copula [bûn].

3.19.1 The Modern Approach

Different explanations have been given by Kurd grammarians and researchers to oppose the traditionalists approach who consider the affixial particles (supposed auxiliaries) [-m,-in,-n-,-n,-a] as contacted forms of the auxiliaries [bun] and [habûn] in the present tense like v.be of English.
Muhammad (1974: 98–99) for instance, denies the existence of affixial forms of [bûn] and [habûn] and states that, "in fact, these are not auxiliaries like the English and French verbs be and have, they are affixial pronominals that do not inflect for time". Dizaīy (1984: 7) approaches this subject analytically and gives his own clarification depending on phonological explanation, stating that: "sometimes the sound [h] is deleted in Kurdish, especially when it is preceded or followed by a vowel sound or when it occurs between them." Such as in:

- *[min birdû ha ma]~ [min birdûma]*

- *[min henāw ha ma]~ [min henāwma]*

Moreover, Ahmed (1988: 63) states that, "there is an implied auxiliary [bûn] and/or [habûn]. They have been assimilated and deleted through the repeated use and via phonological changes of the verbs", thus:

- *[mārek la kûnakadāy a]* was originally *[mārek la kunakadā haya]*.

He adds that there are no verbless sentences in Kurdish, like any other live languages. In order to recognize [bûn] as auxiliary verbs, grammarians and researchers like Ali Amin (1986), Yosopova (1987), Ahmed (1988), Fakhri (1994), Alani (1985), Marif (2000) and Musa (2000) have different insights to indicate the position(s) in which the verb [bûn] is to be considered as an auxiliary. These views can be summed up as follows:
  a. When [bun] is followed by a prepositional phrase (prep.):

- *[aw bû ba māmostā]* (He became a teacher). In this its basic meaning is 'to exist' and shows changing of state.

  b. When it co-occurs with a noun to form compound verbs.

- *[zard bû]*, it became (turned into) yellow.

  c. When it is attached to another verb having the inf. form:

- *[hāt bû]*, he/she had come.

In all the three above cases the verb [bûn] relatively loses its basic meaning and conveys other meanings like *become* and it only shows past time (i.e., it is shows time).

However, Fakhri (1995: 36) considers the type of verbs that help the formation of complex verbs as auxiliary verbs, such as [hałbû]. But if this is an auxiliary, it must be empty semantically according to the definition of Ma'ruf (1989: 48), that auxiliaries are empty words semantically. Moreover, the particles that are attached to them are also meaningless. So, how can one predict the meaning of these verbs in this case? It is concluded that [bûn] is not considered an auxiliary in this position.

3.20 OTHER AUXILIARY VERBS

In their definition of auxiliary verbs, Fakhri and Mukiriani (1982:154) conceive of auxiliary verbs as those verbs that have binary functions; as a main verb and as an auxiliary that combine with other grammatical elements like

N. adj, adv. to form compound verbs (mentioned before). Kurdoev (1982: 220) also states that verbs like [bun, dān, hatin, hayen] fall under auxiliary verbs. Ma'ruf (1989:48–52) expands the notion stating that all the verbal elements that help to compose compound verbs are auxiliary verbs. They are (relatively) empty, stressless verbs that are capable of inflection to show tense, aspect, mood and voice. Moreover, they can function as main verbs when they are the only verb in a sentence.

Generally, auxiliary verbs derive from full verbs. The most likely verbs to become auxiliary verbs are stative verbs (such as be, sit, and stand), *simple* verbs of *motion* (such as go) and finally *complement-taking* verbs (such as say, finish, etc.). In Kurdish, the auxiliary verbs are derived from the first two types mentioned above, i.e., *state* and *motion verbs*.

Accordingly, Ma'ruf (1989:48–52) categorises this second group of auxiliary verbs, i.e., [hātin, henān, dān, etc.] into two major types: eventive and state verbs. Eventive verbs indicate an event, action and movement from the part of the subject. They are verbs like [kird, girt, dā, kawt, xwārd, henā], which are combined with the preceding nominal element (that may be preceded by a preposition or not) to form a verbal element. Hence, the verbal element is called 'compound eventive', (ibid, 1989: 48).

State auxiliary verbs include a number of verbs especially an implied (deleted) [bûn, habûn] and several other verbs like [kird, hāt, hałgaŕā, kawt] that indicate the state of their subject, (ibid: 1989: 51). They are collocated with the former adj. or adv. or N.

- *[ciyāi b karawa]* imperative
- *[ciyāi kird awa]* past
- *[ciyāi da ka mawa]* present
- *[ciyāi da kird awa]* imperfect
- *[ciyāi bi kird ayawa]* subjunctive
- *[ciyāi kira tyawa]* passive

On the other hand, Marif (2000:267–270) and Amedy (1978: 232–235) prove the auxiliariness of this verb group by referring to their role in passivization and when followed by an inf. in Northern dialect. Both grammarians prove that [bûn, habûn, kirdin, dān] and Marif adds [henā, kawtin, xistin] help in the formation of passive voices when they are attached to another main verb.

- *[az hātim girtne]* (I was caught).

But in the Southern dialect (henceforth, SD) [hātin], which is the intransitive form of [henān] and [hānīn], is rarely used as an auxiliary. It is not used for passivization, whereas [henān] and [hānin] (the transitive forms) can act as an auxiliary actively and help to change a number of verbs from intransitive into transitive rather than for the formation of passive voices, (Marif, 1992: 13) and (Marif, 2002: 269).

- *[aw dahenma pekanin]* I make him laugh.
- *[aw mini dā ba girtin]* He made me caught.
- *[āmnji xista giriān]* He made Amanj cry.
- *[hamû lašim hāta larzīn]* All my body come to tremble.
- *[lašim kawta larzīn]* My body come to tremble.

3.21 FUNCTION OF THE AUXILIARIES

The function of auxiliary verbs is that they express 'auxiliary information', such as tense, aspect or mode', (Payne, 1997: 82). In Kurdish, both groups of auxiliaries are used to convey this information.

The second group of auxiliaries like [hāt, xwārd, kawt, henā, etc.] including the implied [būn] and [habûn], which are essential elements of compound verbs are used to form tense, aspect and mood of compound verbs. Kurdoev (1982: 220) states this fact but points to only [bun, hatin, hayne, dān].

Fakhri (1996:11) identifies three major functions of auxiliary verbs in Kurdish, she does refer to their major function which is their participation in aspect and mood but she concentrates on that, that these verbs (i.e.,auxiliary verbs) help the formation of compound and complex words, moreover they help in the formation of sentences which lack an event verb.

Another function of this auxiliary verb group is reflected in their participation of passive voice. In Northern dialect this group, especially [hatin, dān, bûn and kirdin] help the formation of passive voice, (Amedy, 1978: 323–325). Similarly, [bûn] and [habûn], i.e., the first auxiliary group helps in the formation of variety of tenses, aspects and as they can be inflected for both types of tenses (present and past) and show aspects and mood.

Soane (1913: 42–28) identifies a number of functions (uses of tenses as he claims, because he did not distinguish between tense and aspect) that can be expressed via [bûn] and [habûn]. The most recognizable functions identified by Soane (ibid, 1913: 42–28) are: Present indicative, Pretrite, Perfect, Pluperfect, Subjunctive and Optative, Conditional, Imperative.

However, one can summarize all the functions that can be conveyed via [bûn] and [habûn] by summing all those functions given by Ali Amin (1986: 242), Musa (2000:9) Ma'ruf (1989) Marif (2000), Fakrhri (1995) and taking Baban's (1997) as the frame, as he approaches the subject more precisely and analytically he considers all *past forms* as derived forms supported by the auxiliary, (ibid, 1997: 14).

1. Auxiliaries in the Present

(Indicative mood)
a. Near past:

- *mn [kawt[]m] I fell*
- *to [kawt[]it] you fell*
- *ema [kawt[]in] we fell*
- *ewa [kawt[]in] you fell*
- *awan [kawt[]n] they fell*

b. Past imperfect:

- dakawt [ ] m I was falling
- dakwt []it you were falling
- dakawt[]in, etc. they were falling

2. Auxiliaries in the Past
a. Past perfect: [kawtbu] *he/she/it had fallen*
b. Pluperfect:

- *[kawt []*, *fell*
- *[nārdûma] I have sent*
- *[kawt[b]m] I would have fallen*
- *[kawt[b]it] you would have fallen*
- *[kawt[b]in] you(sg) would have fallen*
- *[kawt[b]n] you(pl) would have fallen*
- *[kawt[b]n] they would have fallen*

3. Past subjunctive:

- *[bubim] I became*
- *[bubam] I would have been*
- *[bubamay] I would have become*

3.22 MOOD

Traditionally mood is said to express the speakers' attitude to a 'proposition or to its truth-value', (Dahl, 1985: 26). In Kurdish, mood reflects "the relationship of the action or state expressed by the verb to reality as conceived by the speaker: real versus unreal", (McCarus, 1958: 61). The majority of grammarians agree that mood is the characteristic of verbs in Kurdish, i.e. mood is expressed by verbs, but there are others like Mahwi (2007)[6] who views mood as the characteristic of the whole sentence rather of verbs.

Ahmed (2005: 10) points to three methods for expressing mood in Kurdish. Thus, mood is of three types in his opinion: lexically (via verbs), which includes indicative, conditional and imperative mood, formal (by form) such as the use of 'modality and modal auxiliaries' and finally by modulation such by exclamatory and interrogative sentences.

Based on the former view, Kurdish verbs have various types of mood. Each mood has its own form and purpose of use. Grammarians classify moods differently such as McCarus (1958: 61), Marif (2000: 185) Nabaz (1976:37), Amin (1979: 49–53). Ultimately, it can be stated that four types of mood is found in Kurdish: Indicative, Conditional, and Imperative and subjunctive mood. Since only subjunctive mood is of concern here, it will be explained in the following section.

3.22.1 Subjunctive Mood

Subjunctive names an unreal type of action; it expresses such concepts like wish, suggestion, request, suspension, etc., (Yosopova, 1987: 85). McCarus (1958: 62) points out that, verbs in subjunctive mood appears either alone or as an element in a large utterance. When it appears alone as an entire utterance; it conveys a 'deliberative' such as [biĉim] (shall I go) or 'factitive' such as [biĉe] (make him go) meanings, (ibid, 1958: 61–62). But Bomba (2001: 89) argues that this verb can not be used alone in utterances. It can be used with other grammatical categories and verbs that demand a subjunctive verb; together they convey the modal meanings of the utterance.

In negation [na-] substitutes [b/bi]. Verbs in subjunctive mood occur in both types of tenses and all types of aspects in the language. However, in compounds the prefix [bi-] is optional in the present subjunctive.

- *[bāng bikam]~[bāng kam]* I call

This omission regularly takes place with those compound verbs that are introduced with the prefix [war-] and [hał-], (Thackston, 2006: 30):

- *[war bigret]~[war gret]* receive

3.23 MODALITY EXPRESSIONS

Studies on Kurdish grammar and especially those in the field of mood and modal verbs are controversial in terms the existence of modal verbs. On one hand, Amin (1979: 109–110) in his work on modal verbs ,which is considered the fist work in this area, assumes that there are three modal verbs in Kurdish which are [bûn],(when it occurs in the 3rd sg), [twānīn] and[werān]. He proves this assumption by setting five criteria of auxiliary verbs such as:

their dependence to the following main verb, and occupying the left position them (of the main verb), the inability to combine the *modal* with the main verb with the conjunction [w] 'and', no sequencing of auxiliary verbs and finally, "the main verb with the modal is always marked for present subjunctive", (Amin, 1979: 110).

On the other hand, Bomba (2001:78–88) concludes that Kurdish/Central dialect (Sulaimani dialect) does not have modal verbs for expressing modality, and that Kurdish verbs are unlike English and German auxiliaries in their behaviour in negation, interrogation, elliptic, inflection, question-tags. So, she labels them Verbs That Demand Subjunctive Verbs. Similarly, Mahwi (2007) [7] has the same point of view.

Furthermore, Ahmed (2005: 6) confirms that in Northern dialect no sign of modal auxiliary verbs However, there are alternative linguistic means. He labels them Modal Forms as a general term. If these verbs are located in other contexts, i.e., not followed by subjunctive verbs, they do not convey modal meanings, but function as any lexical verb.

In the present study, those linguistic means that are used to express modal meanings in Kurdish are classified linguistically, following the classification by Huddleston and Pullum (2002: 173–175), as follows:

1. Lexical modals: it includes such grammatical categories like certain verbs [pewista, dabet, dabwāya, datwānet, etc], adverbs such as [kātek, pāšān, īnjā, etc.] and NPs such as [pewsta, nāĉār] and adjectives like [ranga] that all are followed by a subjunctive complement.

Verbs are completed with subjunctive verbs or that demand subjunctive verbs are a number of uninflected, regular verbs that have subjunctive verbal complements; together with the verb they convey variety of modal meanings. These verbs are like [dabet, twānīn, wistin, ḥazkirdin, ārazû kirdin, werān, zānīn, peĉun, bo lwān, damawet, hełān, etc]. Semantically they are equal to English central modals and syntactically they are also equal to them as they can function as main and auxiliary verbs, (Bomba, 2001: 106). They have certain formal features that give them this status, as follows:

    a. They can be inflected for all types of tenses and aspects.

    b. All of them are citation forms that all have an affective role in the syntactic structure of the language.

    c. When they occur alone, they are meaningless unless they co-occur with the following verb in a sentence.

- *[min dabet] I have to.
- *[min dabet birom]* I have to go.

    d. Usually they initiate the VP, (ibid: 2001: 106). Ahmed (2005: 6) states that these verbs fall outside the domain of the simple sentence to show the attitude of the speaker. Their being in this position indicates that these verbs not auxiliaries. The auxiliary verb are verbs which help or support the main verb to form a verbal phrase, (ibid, 2005: 6).

- *[damawet qisat lagal bikam]* I want to talk to you.

  e. These is no a sequence of them in the utterance.

- *[min dabet datwanin ḥazdakam birom]

  f. They are not combined with the following word with a conjunction.

- *[damawet w brom bo darawa]

  g. Most of them are completed by subjunctive verbs.

- *[dabet bixoiy la gaḷmana]* you must eat with us.

h. They govern the time and aspect of the following subjunctive verb. For instance [dabû], which is past continuous is followed by a verb in Past continuous subjunctive, Past(Pretrite) and Present subjunctive:

Note standing, not all verbs behave in the same manner in this concern. Each obeys a certain rule; for instance [damtwānī] which is similarly past continuous as [dabet] (cf), but it is to be followed a verb in present (in all its aspects) subjunctive and or in past continuous indicative.

2. Subordination: There is a "significant association between subordination and markers of modality", (Huddleston and Pullum, 2002: 174). In Kurdish, usually the subordinate clause is linked with the main clause via a number of clause connectors, such as conjunctions. Some times verbs in the matrix clause would be subjunctive depending on the type of the conjunctions used.

Since Kurdish is one of the languages that enjoys a high inflectional system, subjunctive verbs play a crucial role in conveying the modal meanings. Huddleston and Pullum (2002: 174) point out this fact by stating: "in languages with inflectional subjunctive ... this mood characteristically indicates non-factuality in subordinate clauses".

In order to understand different kinds of subordinate clauses, it is essential to know the different kinds of conjunctions which combine subordinate clauses to the main clause. McCarus (1958: 100) points out that conjunctions in Kurdish occur either in single utterances that consist of a single clause which he labels them 'independent connectors' such as:

- *[bā]-[bā bŕoin]* Let's go.
- *[baškim], [baḷkû]-[baḷlkû /baškim ben]* May they come.

64   Chapter 3

Or they may occur in clauses that consist of more than one clause labelled as 'subordinate connectors', (ibid: 1958: 100).

Consistent with the above notion of subordinate connectors, Shwani (2003: 24) identifies a number of these conjunctions (though he labels them with the term Relative Particles) that occur in complex sentences forming different types of subordinate clauses such as: nominal, adjectival, adverbial, conditional, contrast, negative, objectival, wish and suspension subordinate clauses (nominal and adjectival subordinations are out of the scope of the present study).

3.24 MODAL MEANINGS

The verbs and different linguistic categories explained can be used to convey different types of meanings as indicated in table 3.1.

Lexical modals can be used to convey the same kinds of all meanings: epistemic, denotic and dynamic meanings as in table 3.2.

Table 3.1. Modal Meanings.

Modal meanings	verbs	Conjunctions Interrogations
Desire and wish	[haz dakam, wistin, xozga xwastin]	[xozga]
Permission: Asking permission	[māwa habûn, rega pedān, twānīn]	
Giving permission	[twānīn, bo habûn]	
Reason	[bo awai]	
Suggestion and recommendation	[pešniāz kirdin],[bastir waya,	[bā,da bā,da sā]
Necessity and obligation	[pewist bun, dabet]	
Possibility	[pe dacet]	[ranga,lawaya]
Probability	[wā dānān, wā boĉûn,šiān]	
Habit	[wā fahātw]	
comparison		
Offer	[Twānin,]	
threats		Da, da, bā
Prediction or deduction	[twānin, wā hast kirdin, wā bo ĉun, peĉun, pešbini kirdin]	[lawanya]
Advice and recommendation	[pewist bûn, bas bûn, wā bāštira ,etc]	[bā,tā,hatāhataku,bo awai,labar awai]
Ability	[twānin,la bārdā bûn, hez habûn etc]	[awanda, ka awanda, ka,henda, jā]
Condition		[hatā, hatawāku, bo awai, agar,ka]
Intention	[niāz bûn, hatin]	[tā, hatā, hatāku,bo awai]
promise	[gift dān, hān dān]	[har, marja]
preference	[pe xoš bûn]	
Request	[twānīn]	
Apologizing	[twānīn]	

In sum, it can be concluded that in the Kurdish language two groups of auxiliary verbs are observed that perform the primary functions of verbs, i.e., showing tense, aspect and voice. [bûn] and [habûn] represent the first group, which occur independently (not attached to non-verbal elements) but having different allomorphs according to their grammatical contexts. The second group of primary auxiliaries appear dependent or attached to certain non-verbal elements; similarly to convey the same primary functions in the language.

Table 3.2. Kinds of Modality Expressed by the Lexical Modals.

Types of modality Lexical Modals	Epistemic	Denotic	Dynamic
[pe xos bûn, [haz kirdin]			[pem xoša /haz dakam sardanmān bikait] I would like you to visit us.
[wīstin]		[damawet hič nałeit] I don't want you to say any thing	
[fega pedān]		[fegam dadait bema žûrawa?] May I come in?	
[twānīn]	[datwanit la taqi kirdnawaka da bicit] you can pass the exam.	datwanit biroit You can leave.	datwanim yarmatit bidam. I can help you.
[bo habûn]		[bot haya qisa bikait] You can speak.	
[niāz habun]			[niāzim wāya bifrom] I want to leave.
[tā,hatā]	[hātim tā bitbinim] I came till I see you.		
[bo away]	[dačim bo awai bībinim] I go so as I can see him.		
[pešniaz kirdin]	[pesniaz dakam ka broin] I suggest we go.		
[bā, dabā]		[bā brion] Let's go.	
[pewist bûn]		[pewista xot piāāni pizisk bidait] you must see the doctor.	
[dabet]	dabet bibāret? Do you think it will rain?	dabet beit la gałim. You must come with me.	

Auxiliary Verbs in English 67

[ba xayāɫdā hatin]	[wā hast dakam taqi kirdinawaka bibrit] I feel you will pass the exam.	
[pe daĉet]/lawa daĉet/dagunjet]	[lawa daĉet aw bet] it seems that it is him.	
[wā bāštira[		[wa bastira la kitebxana bixwenitawa]. It is better for you to study in the library.
[ranga,lawānaya,wāai bo daĉim,pe daĉet]	Lawanaya/ranga/wai bo dacim aw bet I think its him.	
[wā dānān,wā zanin,wa bocun]	[wai bo dacim/dazaninim/hast dakam ka ben] I predict they will come.	
[wa rahatin]		[wa rahatwa zw la xaw haste] he used to get up early
[bawar kirdin]		Bawar nakam henda hazar bin
[gar, agar]	[gar bixweni,dardaci] if you study, you will pass.	
[la barda bun, hez ahbu]		[hici labarda nia,hic hezi nia] he can not do anything.
[weran]		[nawerim ba tanha birom] I don't dare to go alone.
[mawa habûn]	[mawa haya walam bidamawa?] Am I to answer?	
[Baɫen dān][gifit dān]	[balen/gifit dadam la qisat darnaĉim] I promise to obey you.	
[awanda]	[awanda birom mandu dabim].	]awanda male] don't say a lot.

	if I walk so much I will get tired.	
[kātek]		[Katek dem aw la mal nabet] I come when he is not home.
[hatākû]	[hataku hawil nadait darnacit] unless you try hard, you wont succeed.	
[wak aw/wā]	[tos wak aw bit,minci bikam] if you look like him, what should I do?	
[bałkû]	[balku kas w kari binasetawa]. May his relatives recognize him.	

In Kurdish different attitudes of the speaker towards the factuality or actualization of a proposition of the speaker are expressed by a number of lexical and syntactic realizations with subjunctive verbs as main components in their complementation, but not with modal auxiliaries. The modal meanings which are expressed are like necessity, probability, possibility, suggestions, permission, advice, etc. Thus, all the three types of modal meanings like epistemic, denotic and dynamic are found in Kurdish.

NOTES

1. The Auxiliary in this sense, which involves a set of lexical items, is not the same as AUX, which was hypothesized by Transformational Grammar (henceforth, TG). In this sense, AUX refers to an abstract category which was supposed to be present in sentences universally and which serves as the locus for certain grammatical categories, such as tense. Later in GB it has been replaced by INFL, which also serves the same function, (Trask, 993: 24).

2. Fintel (2006: 2) distinguishes different kinds of modal meaning. Alethic modality (Greek: aletheia, meaning 'truth'), sometimes logical or metaphysical modality, concerns what is possible or necessary in the widest sense. Epistemic modality (Greek episteme). Deontic modality (Greek: deon, meaning 'duty'). Bouletic modality, sometimes boulomaic modality, concerns what is possible or necessary, given a person's desires. Circumstantial modality, sometimes dynamic modality, concerns what is possible or necessary, given a particular set of circumstances. Teleological modality (Greek telos, meaning 'goal') concerns what means are possible or necessary for achieving a particular goal.

3. Epistemic modality is sometimes labeled as 'evidential' since it is often based on evidence.

4. The modals used in the necessity sense indicate a knowledge that the speaker arrived at by inference and reasoning rather than by direct experience. Thus, statements as *you must be tired/Ivan* convey a knowledge acquired by direct experience rather by inference. In this sense, according to Leech (1971:72), logical necessity is weakened to logical assumption.

5. In the literature, other terms have been used instead of subjective and objective permission; Leech (1971) for instance, refers to the first type that sort of permission 'given by the speaker'. The term 'general permission' is also used to mean the objective one; that is used in formal contexts without respect to who does the permitting.
6. In an personal interview with Mahwi in 5/23/2007.
7. In a personal meeting with him in 3/23/2007.

Chapter Four

Data Collection

4.1 TEST DESIGN

The test has been designed to assess the subjects' ability at both levels: recognition and production. The test is divided into two parts. It comprises five questions: the first and the second questions are designed to measure the subjects' responses at recognition level whereas the rest of the questions, i.e., the third, the fourth and the fifth are intended to test the subjects' responses at the production level.

The first and the second questions consist of ten (10) items each. The former is designed to assess the subjects' recognition of meanings of different modal auxiliaries by using multiple-choice technique, whereas the latter is designed to test the subjects' recognition of the formal properties of auxiliary verbs: primary and the modals.

The third, the fourth and the fifth questions are designed to measure the subjects' responses at the production level: Question three consists of five items. The technique adopted is that a situation is given and the subjects are required to produce utterances referring to permission, offer, conclusion, non-necessity and preference.

Question four has five (5) items, in which transformational technique is used, i.e., the learner changes the structure in some prescribed manner. This question is only formed to test the subjects' mastery of the syntax of auxiliary verbs, such as inversion, code, emphatic and back shifting.

Question five consists of five (5) items, too. The test procedure being used is translation from the L1, i.e., Kurdish to English.

4.2 THE SAMPLE

The real sample of the present study consists of 190 third year EFL learners of the Colleges of Languages at the Universities of Sulaimani, Saladin and Koya and 40 EFL learners of third year at the Colleges of Basic Education at the universities of Sulaimani and Saladin during the academic year (2007–2008). Thus the total is 190 EFL learners.

All the learners are native speakers of Kurdish with relatively similar EFL background and their average age is between (20–21) years old. They represent both sexes and are chosen haphazardly. Learners from other countries like Syria and Iran were excluded from the sample as it is thought they have got a different Kurdish dialect (especially the Syrians).

The third year University learners are chosen as the sample of the test as they are believed to be advanced and qualified in the area of English auxiliary verbs. All the testees have been given the topic in their second year of their studies of university. The textbooks adopted in their second years are Basic Grammar in Use by Murphy and Smazler (2003) and English Grammar in Use by Murphy (1994).

4.3 TEST OBJECTIVES

Measurement is a requirement for every scientific experimentation, and language tests are measuring instruments "meant to measure the learners knowledge of the language," (Corder, 1973: 367). Carroll (1968: 48) provides the following definition of a test: "a psychological or educational test is a procedure designed to elicit certain behaviour from which one can make inferences about certain characteristics of an individual."(cited in Bachman, 1990: 20). In plain words, it is a "method of measuring a person's ability or knowledge in a given area." (Brown: 1987: 218)

Language testing is classified differently according to different distinctive features. Bachman (1990: 70), for instance, points out five types of these features: the purpose for which they are intended, the content upon which they are based, the frame of reference within which their results are based, the way of scoring and the specific technique or method they employ.

According to different purposes that tests provide, Brown (1987: 225) mentions four types of language tests; proficiency, diagnostic, achievement and aptitude tests. Since the objective of this study is to investigate Kurdish students' mastery of English auxiliary verbs, a diagnostic test has been thought appropriate to identify learners' strengths and weaknesses since such test are "intended primarily to ascertain what learning still needs to take place."(Hughes, 2003: 15). Diagnostic test types are "devices for provoking the learner into showing what he knows, what his interlanguage is.", (Corder,

1973: 367). Thus, the test of the present study is intended to demonstrate how well the learners mastered the material, i.e., the syntactic and semantic aspects of English auxiliary verbs and analyze the results then draw conclusions and suggestions since the main objective of a test is to provide feedback and since testing is associated with making of decisions, (Baker, 1989: 3).

4.4 TEST MERITS

All good tests are characterized by two major virtues or merits; validity and reliability.

4.4.1 Test validity

The most important quality of test interpretation or use is validity. Validity is "the extent to which the test measures what is supposed to measure and nothing else" (Heaton, 1988: 159). Validity is concerned with the question: how much of an individuals' performance is due to the language abilities we want to measure and with maximizing the effects of these abilities on test scores, (Bachman: 1990: 161). Added to this, Lado (1961: 30) argues that "validity can be achieved and verified by correlating the scores of a test with those of another test or criterion which is valid."

Two types of validity are taken into consideration in the present study: content validity and face validity. On one hand, Anastasti (1982: 131) defines content validity as "essentially the systematic examination of the test content to determine whether it covers a representative sample of the behaviour domain to be measured", (cited in weir, 1990: 25). Content validity is important in that respect as the greater the test's content validity the more likely it is to be an accurate measure of what is supposed to measure. (Hughes, 2003: 27).

On the other hand, a test is said to have face validity if a test item looks right to other testers, teachers, moderators and testees, (Heaton, 1988: 159) (cf. Harries, 1969: 21) and "it looks as if it measures what is supposed to measure.", (Hughes 2003: 33). Thus, face validity refer, not to exactly what the test actually measures but to what it appears to be superficially measuring.

Though Farhadi, Jafrpoor and Birjandi (1994), Bachman (1990), Hughes (2003) discount the value of face validity, yet Farhadi, Jafrpoor and Birjandi (1994: 150) go further and consider it a desirable feature from a public opinion and should not be underestimated. Besides, Hughes (2003: 33), who views the term not scientific, stresses the fact that if a test lacked face validity it may simply not be used.

The present research instrument (, i.e., the test) has been exposed to a jury of experts who has given their suggestions and recommendations on each question one by one, such as increasing the item numbers and number of choices, the way the questions are to be organized, even on modifying test instructions. For achieving the face validity of the test and fulfill the purpose which is designed for, their suggestions have been taken into account as items has been deleted, modified and added.

4.4.2 Test Reliability

A fundamental criterion by which language tests have to be judged is their reliability. Reliability is a "quality of test scores which refers to the consistency of measures across different times, tests, forms, raters, and other characteristics of the measurement context."(Mousavi, 1999: 323). On the same line, Madsen (1983: 179) argues that a reliable test is one that produces essentially the same results consistently on different occasions when the conditions of the test remain the same. Accordingly, a reliable test is a test that is consistent and dependable, (Brown, 1987: 220). Reliability is so essential in a test that without it the results cannot be believed, furthermore it is related to validity that it is useless the test is valid.

There are several methods by which reliability can be estimated. Brown (1988: 99) points to three major ways by which test reliability is measured: test-retest, the use of parallel forms and internal consistency. Internal consistency can be measured in a number of ways: split-half method, Kuder-Richardson 20 and Cronbach alpha a. internal consistency estimates are most often used in language studies because "they have the distinct advantage of being estimable from a single form of a test administered only once," (ibid: 1988: 99). This approach is based on the number of items and the variance of the test. The formula is:

$a = k/k-1(1-\sum S^2 i/S^2 X)$

Where k=the number of items.

$\sum S^2 i$=the sum of the variance of the different parts of the test.

$S^2 X$=the variance of the test score (Mousavi, 1999:44)

For this study, the latter method, i.e., Cronbach alpha a have been performed by using SPSS computer program, by which reliability for each question is found out separately. The computation of this formula has yielded that the reliability coefficient of each question is as follows:

The first question=0.945
The 2nd question=0.945
The 3rd question=0.983
The 4rh question=0.877
The 5th question=0.977

From the results one recognizes that the testis of highly positive correlation which is near to 1:00, i.e., the reliability of an ideal test in which the test would give precisely the same results for a particular set of candidates without regard of when it was when it was administrated, (Hughes, 2003:39). Moreover, this range of numbers fall under what Lado (1961) expects for good language tests including tests of structure which their reliability are usually in the .90 to .99 range, (cited in Hughes, 2003: 39)

4.5 PILOT TESTING

Educational methodology stipulates that a newly written test material is to go through a pretest or a pilot test before publication, development, and operational administration to determine their suitability and effectiveness and to the reactions of the testees to the materials. This sort of test is usually administrated to a relatively small group of learners before applying it to the real sample. Thus, pilot tests are carried out to uncover any problems, and to address is an important means of assessing the feasibility and usefulness of the data collection methods and making any necessary revisions before they are used with the research participants. (Mackey and Gass, 2005: 43).

Accordingly, for the purpose of the present study a pilot test was given to twenty five college students from College of Languages/University of Sulaimani on the 16th of December 2007. The subjects were chosen randomly. This try out aimed at determining the required time for answering the total items, checking out whether the test items need modification, deletion or further clarification and recognizing the subjects comprehension of the test instructions.

As a result of observation, about an hour is considered necessary for responding the entire items of the test. Furthermore, the results obtained from this test had been incorporated to the final version of the test.

4.6 SELECTION OF THE TEST MATERIAL

Some items of this test have been picked from various practical grammar books such as English Language Tests by W.S. Fowler and Norman Coe (1976), Grammar Practice Activities by Penny Ur (1988), Advanced Language Practice by Michael Vince (1994), Fundamentals of English Grammar by Betty Schramfer Azar (2003), English Grammar in Use by Raymond Murphy (1994), Longman English grammar Practice by Alexander L.G (1990) and a number of grammatical books mentioned in chapter three. The items cover the syntactic and semantic aspects of different types of auxiliary verbs in English in general. Furthermore, the test has been submitted to a jury[1] committee of eight university lecturers whose recommendations and suggestions have been taken into consideration.

4.7 FINAL ADMINISTRATION

After ensuring the test's reliability and validity qualifications, the main test was administered on the 26th, 27th, 28th, 30th, and 31st January at the Colleges of Languages and Basic Education in Koya, Saladin and Sulaimani during the academic year 2007–2008.

The time required for the whole test has proved to be an hour. The subjects were motivated to respond as spontaneously and seriously as possible. The instructions were explained clearly for them and necessary directions and explanations were given to them. Furthermore, they were given the chance to ask for any clarification or explanation they might need.

4.8 THE SCORING SCHEME

An explicit scoring scheme has been performed to make the test reliable. The whole test has been scored out of 100. Each item is scored either correct or incorrect. Each correct item of the 1st and 2nd questions is assigned 2.30 scores, while 3 scores are assigned to each item in the 3rd and 4rh questions. Finally, correct items of question 5 are given 4 scores each. Zero score is assigned to an item that is answered incorrectly or even not answered by the subject. Such items indicate that the subjects have failed to give any answer.

The scoring scheme for the present study can be illustrated in table 4.1.

4.9 STATISTICAL MEANS

4.9.1 Measures of Central Tendency

Mode, median, and mean are all measures of central tendency.

4.9.1.1 Mode

Mode is the easiest measure of central tendency. It is "the score that occurs most frequently in a set of scores." (Brown, 1988: 67). The mode of the present study test is 40.

4.9.1.2 Median

Median is defined as the "score at the center of the distribution—that is, the score that splits the group in half."(Mackey and Gass, 2005: 254). The me-

Table 4.1. The Scoring Scheme

No. of Questions	No. of Items	Scores	Percentage %
1	10	25	25
2	10	25	25
3	5	15	15
4	5	15	15
5	5	20	20
Total	35	100	100

dian can be found by putting all the individual scores in order of magnitude and choosing the middle one. The median of the present test is (39.5)

4.9.1.3 Mean

The most common measure of central tendency is Mean. Hughes (2003: 220) states that "the mean is simply the average of all the scores made on the test". The mean can be found by the following formula:

$X^- = \sum X/N$
X^- = the mean
X=raw scores (Mousavi, 1999: 214)
$\sum$ = the sum

Thus, the mean for the present test is (40.03684).

4.9.2 Measures of Dispersion

The mean by itself does not always give an appropriate summery of a set of scores. This is because different sets of scores may give the same mean. So, what is needed is an indication of the ways the scores are distributed around the mean. This can be achieved via standard deviation (SD). The standard deviation is "a number that shows how scores are spread around the mean." (Mackey and Gass, 2005: 259) or it is "a sort of average of the differences of all scores from the mean." (Brown, 1988: 69)

It is the square root of the average, square distance of the scores from the mean, i.e., the square root of the variance. The formula is:

$SD = \sqrt{\sum X^2/N-1}$
X=the score minus the mean (Mousavi, 1999:362)
N= the number of items
$\sum$ =the sum

The D of the present study is (12.11332)

NOTE

1. The jury committee included:
Prof. Dinha Tobia Gorgis (Ph.D. in Linguistics), / Jadara University for Graduate Studies, Jordan.
Asst Prof. Basim Y. Jasim (Ph.D. in Applied Linguistics)/ College of Arts/ University of Mosul.
Asst Prof. Munthir Manhal Muhammad (Ph.D. in Linguistics), College of Languages / University of Baghdad.
Asst. Prof. Muhammad Mahwi (Ph.D. in General Linguistics and Kurdish Language, College of Languages / University of Sulaimani.
Ass Prof. Riyadh Khalid Ibrahim (Ph.D. in Linguistics), College of Languages/ University of Baghdad.
Ass Prof. Nidham Shit Hamid (Ph.D. in Linguistics), College of Arts / University of Baghdad.
Ass Prof. Wais Chalwd Ibrahim, (Ph.D. in Linguistics), College of Basic Education/ University of Mosul.
Dr. Suhair Safwat Mohammed Hashim, (Ph.D. in Linguistics), College of Languages/ University of Sulaimani)

Chapter Five

Data Analysis and Discussion of the Results

5.1 DISCUSSION OF THE RESULTS

The analysis of the achieved data is of importance since it will be the basis upon which the researcher's hypotheses mentioned in (1.3) will either be verified or refuted.

5.2 QUANTITATIVE ASSESSMENT

5.2.1 The Subjects' Performance in the Recognition Test

The first question is constructed to measure the subjects' performance in recognizing different modal meanings. Table 5.1 presents the results obtained after analyzing the subjects' performance at each item in this question.

As it is clear from the table 5.1 the number and percentage of correct responses is (1036, 55%) which is higher than that of the incorrect answers including the avoided ones is (864, 45%).

These results denote that most of the subjects can infer different modal meanings. This is an indication that not all Kurd learners lack knowledge of the modal meanings, though 45% of them face difficulty in this area. The second question is designed to measure the subjects' performance in comprehending the syntactic properties of English auxiliary verbs. Table (5.2) shows the subjects responses to the items of the second question, as demonstrated below.

The number and percentage of correct responses is (1268, 67%) in contrast with the incorrect ones (including the avoided ones) is (622,

Table 5.1. Frequencies and Percentage of the Subjects' Performance Question (1)

Items	No. of correct responses	%	No. of Incorrect responses	%	Avoided items	%
1	133	70%	57	30%	/	0%
2	53	28%	135	71%	2	1%
3	137	72%	51	27%	2	1%
4	105	55%	80	42%	5	3%
5	91	48%	95	50%	4	2%
6	177	93%	13	7%	/	0%
7	80	42%	98	52%	12	6%
8	115	61%	74	39%	1	1%
9	81	43%	109	57%	/	0%
10	64	34%	122	64%	4	2%
Total	1036	55%	834.00	43%	4.39	2%

33%).These results indicate the fact that most of the testees are able to recognize different forms of English auxiliary verbs.

5.2.2 Comparison of Q1 and Q2 Results

In order to compare the means of Q1 and Q2, a T-test has been used. T-test is a procedure used to compare two samples or data. Accordingly, the following results have been arrived at.

The results indicate that there is a statically significant difference between the means of the two samples, i.e., Q1 and Q2. The mean or average of the second question is (127.8) which is higher than that of the first question, which is (103.6). This indicates that the testees' performance in the second question is higher than that of the first question, i.e., the testees' proficiency in recognizing the forms of English auxiliaries is higher than their proficiency in recognizing the meanings of the auxiliaries. Thus, the second hypothesis which states that the ability of Kurd learners' achievement in recognizing the syntactic aspects of English auxiliaries is higher than their ability in recognizing the meaning of the auxiliaries has been verified.

Additionally, this hypothesis has also been verified by comparing the coefficient variation, (henceforth, C. V.) of the two samples. The results indicated that the C.V. of the first question is (0.298) which is lower than that of the second question is (0. 364), as shown in figure (5.1), with the statical results in table (5.3).

Table 5.2. Frequency and Percentage of the Subjects' Performance Question (2)

No. of items	No. of Correct responses	%	No. of Incorrect responses	%	No. of avoided items	%
1	126	66%	62	33%	2	1.1%
2	172	91%	18	9%	/	/
3	183	96%	6	3%	1	0.5%
4	137	72%	49	26%	4	2.1%
5	106	56%	84	44%	/	/
6	145	76%	43	23%	2	1.1%
7	119	63%	64	34%	7	3.7%
8	94	49%	94	49%	2	1.1%
9	143	75%	45	24%	2	1.1%
10	53	28%	136	72%	1	0.5%
Total	1278	67%	601	32%	21	1%

5.2.3 The Subjects' Performance in the Production Test

Part two of the test consists of three questions that include (15) items. Concerning the frequency of errors related to the production level, the majority of the testees' answers are incorrect.

The third question is constructed to test the subjects' proficiency at the production level (see 4.1). Table 5.4 demonstrates the analysis of each item.

The statistical results indicate that the subjects are incompetent in producing the modals when the situation requires producing the appropriate modal verb according to the context. This fact is inferred through the total number and percentage of the correct responses (163, 17%), which is lower than the incorrect ones including the avoided ones, which is (787, 83%).

The fourth question is formed to measure the subjects or testees' performance at the production level. Their performances to the items in Q4 are shown in table 5.5.

The results indicate that the testees face difficulty in producing forms of auxiliaries in negation, interrogation, code, and ellipsis and emphatic, since the total number of incorrect responses is (247, 74%), which is higher in contrast to the correct ones which is (26 %). The fifth question is designed to measure the testees' performance at the production level. These results are shown in table 5.6.

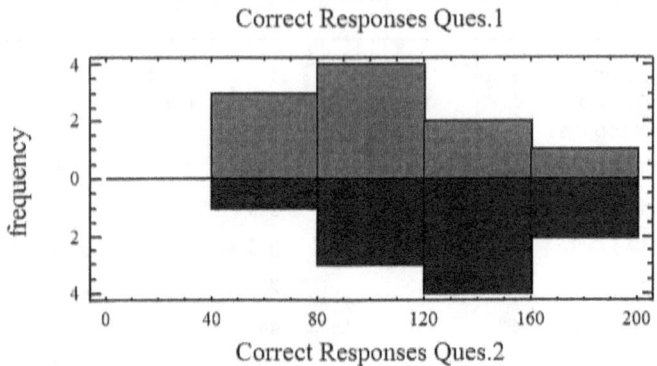

Figure 5.1. Comparing correct responses of Q1 and Q2.

The results indicate that the testees performance at the production level in this question is also low, as indicated by the incorrect responses (including the avoided) which is (83%) as compared with the correct ones (17%).

5.2.4 The Subjects' Performance in the Whole Test

As the results show in table 5.7 the number of the incorrect answers including the avoided ones is (3765, 56.61654%) in contrast with the correct ones which is (2885, 43.38346%). These results show that Kurd EFL learners do not often have full mastery of English auxiliary verbs which verifies the (first) hypothesis that most Kurd EFL university students have difficulty in mastering English auxiliary verbs.

5.2.5 Production vs. Recognition

A comparison of part one and part two of the test in terms of tables and graphs are shown in figure 5.2 and table 5.8 respectively.

The mean for the recognition level of the test (115.7) is markedly higher than that of production level (38.0667). These results verify the (third) hypothesis of the study that the performance of Kurd EFL university students at the recognition level is anticipated to be better than their performance at the production one.

5.3 FACTORS BEHIND LEARNERS' ERRORS

Errors are significant because they are evidence about the nature of the process of foreign language learning and of the rules and categories used by the learner at certain stage in the course, (Corder, 1973:293). Similarly, iden-

Table 5.3. Summary Statistics of Q1 and Q2.

	Sample 1	Sample 2
Count	10	10
Average	103.6	127.8
Variance	1428.27	1433.96
Standard deviation	37.7924	37.8676
Minimum	53.0	53.0
Maximum	177.0	183.0
Range	124.0	130.0
Stnd, skewness	0.801432	-0.674433
Stnd. Kurtosis	0.00603004	0.356906

tifying the source(s) of errors is significant as it leads to an "understanding of how the learners' cognitive and affective self relates to the linguistic system and to formulate an integrated understanding of the process of second language acquisition." (Brown, 1987: 177)

The identification of the exact source of errors my not be completely accurate due to the fact that "many errors are likely to be explicable in terms of multiple rather than single sources." (Ellis and Barkhuizen, 2005:66). Nonetheless, applied linguists like Brown, (1987: 177ff) tend to attribute learner errors to a number of factors; such as inter-lingual transfer, intra-lingual transfer, context of learning, and communication strategies.

5.3.1 Error Taxonomy

In order to classify the errors committed by the testees, a 'surface strategy taxonomy' has been used, which 'highlights the ways surface structures are altered', (Dulay, Burt and Krashen, 1982: 150). The testees omitted, added, misformed, misordered, made mismatching, overgeneralized items. Furthermore, they confused between different meanings of the modals. Accordingly their errors are of omission, addition, misforming, mismatching, misunderstanding, overgeneralizing, misordering which are syntactic errors, whereas errors of confusion occurred in terms of the semantic aspect:

5.3.1.1 Errors with Do

As shown in table 5.9, errors of (1.a and 1.ā) are of omission. The testees tend to omit the main verb *do* whereas the auxiliary is retained in forming negation and question in their sentences. Such errors do not reflect the influence of L1 since the dummy *do* is not used in their mother tongue in forming negation and interrogatives. Thus, it can be interpreted in terms of the opera-

Table 5.4. Frequency and Percentage of the Subjects' Performance Question (3)

No of items	No. of Correct responses	%	No. of Incorrect responses	%	No of Avoided items	%
1	64	34%	123	65%	3	2%
2	15	8%	160	84%	15	8%
3	19	10%	161	85%	10	5%
4	48	25%	131	69%	11	6%
5	17	9%	168	88%	5	3%
Total	163	17%	743	78%	44	5%

tion of incomplete rule application/learning strategy, since the English rule for negation is applied partially. Moreover, such errors are neither of developmental type, which is committed by children nor of L2 learners, since they (children and L2 learners) tend to omit the auxiliary rather than the main verb as (Dulay, Burt and Krashen, 1982: 155) argue, "Language learners omit grammatical morphemes much more frequently than content words". So, they may be the result of 'artifact', (ibid, 1982: 162)

The following samples are examples of such deviant forms:

- *They don't ^ their jobs.
- *What does ken usually ^ on Saturdays?

Errors in (1.b, c, and d) may be due to incomplete rule application. These sorts of errors, i.e., using variables of forms in negation, are observed in the speech of children in one of the acquisition steps of developing negation and also by adult L2 learners. Such errors indicate that learners do no distinguish tense negation in English when the main verb is *do*, i.e., they still require more knowledge of English negation. Examples of such alternating auxiliaries are:

- *They didn't do their jobs.
- *They aren't do their jobs.
- *They haven't do their jobs.

Errors in (1.f), which are additional errors, may be attributed to overuse of a rule as Dulay, Burt and Krashen (1982:56) point out that "additional errors result from the all-too-faithful use of certain rules." An example of such deviant form is:

Table 5.5. Frequency and Percentage of the Subjects' Performance Question (4)

Items	Correct	%	Incorrect	%	Avoided	%
1	114	60%	74	39%	2	1%
2	16	8%	166	87%	8	4%
3	60	32%	86	45%	44	23%
4	17	9%	154	81%	19	10%
5	40	21%	134	71%	16	8%
Total	247	26%	614	65%	89	9%

- *I did helped them.

5.3.1.2 Errors with Be

In table 5.10, Errors in (2.a), i.e., the omission of *be* in elliptical clauses may be attributed to communication strategy/literal translation. In Kurdish elliptical clauses have a different construction; "The enclitic particle-*ash* is added to nouns, noun–adjective phrases and pronoun," (Thackston, 2006:16). Moreover, Kurdish does not have a copula equivalent to the English copula *be*.

Concerning this issue, some linguists and grammarians who wrote on Kurdish grammar like Soane (1913: 80), Mackenzie (1961: 187), Hawramani (1981: 129), Ali Amin (1986: 229) and Faxri (1994: 36) assume that the personal pronouns like [-m,-in,-n-,-a] that are attached to the final ends of the verbal or even nominal group as contracted forms of the auxiliary [bûn] and [habûn] are equivalent to the English copula *be and have*. However, other grammarians and researchers rejected this assumption such as Muhammad (1974: 98–99), Dizaiy (1984: 7), Ahmed (1988: 63), Baban (1997: 4ff) and others and made it clear that these suffixes are personal pronouns rather than auxiliaries and that they are not equivalent to the English *be* and *have*.

As a result of this dissimilarity in structure of both languages, Kurd learners tend to omit *be* in such structures and provide the literal equivalent of the sentence. Thus, such an error is the outcome of communication strategy/literal translation. The sort of the deviant structure that is produced is as the following:

- *Alan is going to school, so ^ his brother.

The deviant form in (2.ā) cannot be considered as an error following the criteria set by Ellis and Barkhuizen (2005: 64) who point out that: "one way to identify errors from mistakes is to check whether the learner alternates

Table 5.6. Frequency and Percentage of the Subjects' Performance Question (5)

Items	Correct	%	Incorrect	%	Avoided	%
1	36	19%	151	79%	3	2%
2	29	15%	156	82%	5	3%
3	74	39%	109	57%	7	4%
4	19	10%	163	86%	8	4%
5	3	2%	180	95%	7	4%
Total	161	17%	759	80%	30	3%

between the erroneous form and the correct target language form". Since this group of testees who committed this deviant form answered the above item (Q2: item3) correctly, i.e., alternated between the deviant and the correct forms, these deviant forms are considered as mistakes.

- *John ^ going to play.

Errors in 2.b can be attributed to L1 interference, since in English passive construction *be* (as an auxiliary) is the protypical auxiliary verb which has no equivalent form in Kurdish. An example of such errors is:

- *The majority of these stories have not written down.

Errors in (3) are additional errors, which are characterized by the presence of an item which must not appear in a well-formed utterance. They are due to exploiting achievement strategy. Learners know that such a structure requires an auxiliary but they are not sure which one is the most suitable. In order to achieve their goal they compensate it with any other auxiliary. Examples of such errors are as follows:

- *Alan is going to school so does his brother.
- *Alan is going to school so will his brother.
- *Alan is going to school so do his brother.

Errors in (4) can be considered as mistakes since the frequency of their occurrence is very low. They may be due to the testees' carelessness or it is the result of the exam pressure. A sample of their mistakes is:

- *Alan is going to school so his brother is.

Table 5.7. Subjects' Whole Achievement at Both Levels

Questions	Correct answers	%	Incorrect answers	%	Avoided ones	%
Q1	1036	55%	834	44%	30	1.6%
Q2	1278	67%	601	32%	21	1%
Q3	163	17%	743	78%	44	5%
Q4	247	26%	614	65%	89	9%
Q5	161	17%	759	80%	30	3%
total	2885	43.38346	3551	53.3985%	214	3.218%

Errors in (5) can be ascribed to the multiplicity of forms of *be* (which was explained in chapter three) which makes learners choose the wrong form in their writings. Examples of such deviant form:

- *Are you writing? *No, I aren't.*

Errors in (6) are due to a number of factors, such as overgeneralization. As a result of his study Ali Abdul Amir (2006: 111) concludes that "The majority of Iraqi EFL university students do not know where weak forms, i.e., WFs occur", they tend to use it in any position thinking that the rule is always true.

It may be also the result of chronological factors (context of learning), since learners have occasionally encountered this form (contracted *be*) in their secondary schools, as *am* is usually introduced in its contracted form in NECI (Shihabi, 1984: 100) they tend to overuse it, ignoring the fact that *"Am, is,* and *are* are not contracted with pronouns in short answers", (Azar, 2003:19).

Examples of such errors:

- **Are you writing? Yes, I'm.*

5.3.1.3 Errors with Have

As shown in table 5.11, errors in (7) can be seen as the result of interference arising from the structural differences between Kurdish and English. Since the question type in which they made the error is translation, transfer occurs. Ellis and Barkhuizen (2005: 38) stress the fact that this device, i.e., translation leads to extensive transfer.

In Kurdish, past perfect is formed inflectionally by attaching the auxiliary [bûn] to another verb having the inf. form: *[hāt bû],* (Ali Amin, 1986: 230), whereas in English this aspect is formed via (had + p.p.). Thus, due to this

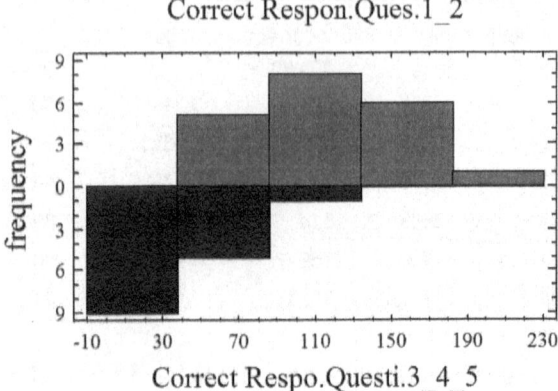

Figure 5.2. Comparing recognition and production results.

opposition interference occurs and the result would be an outsized number of deviant forms as indicated in the table.

Added to this, most of Kurdish grammar text books even grammatical resources (but not all) based on the traditional belief that the Kurdish verb system is essentially based on tense and they recognize a number of tense forms and do not distinguish between tense and aspect, such as Soane (1913), McKenzie (1961), McCarus (1958).

Examples of such errors are as follows:

- *When I arrived the guests have been gone.
- *When I arrived the guests have been going.
- *When I arrived the guests are left.
- *When I arrived the guests have gone.
- *When I arrived the guests went.
- *When I arrived the guests were leave.
- *When I arrived the guests was leaving.

Errors in (8) can be attributed to interference. In Kurdish, invitation is expressed via the subjunctive verb that initiates with [b-] *[biroin]* whereas in English, an offer requires the use of a certain expression that begins with the auxiliary *shall*. So, Kurd learners wrongly place any auxiliary for expressing such an expression as follows:

- *Lets go.
- *May we go?
- *Can we go?

Table 5.8. Summary Statistics of Recognition and Production

	Sample 1	Sample 2
Count	20	15
Average	115.7	38.0667
Variance	1509.91	875.924
Standard deviation	38.8575	29.596
Minimum	53.0	3.0
Maximum	183.0	114.0
Range	130.0	111.0
Stnd. skewness	0.0707456	2.0798
Stnd. kurtosis	-0.678696	1.35729

- *Are we go?*
- *Will we go*
- *Could we go?*
- *Do we go?*

Errors in (9) may be due to interference resulting from the structural dissimilarity between the two languages. Dizaiy (1984: 7–8) argues that one way for the formation of *present perfect* in Kurdish is by the combination of the past participle of a verb with a form of verb [bûn] as an auxiliary (though he uses the term past perfect[1]), whereas the English present perfect is constructed via (have/has+ p.p.). As a result of this, errors occur. The following examples are a handful of those:

- *The majority of these stories haven't being written down.*
- The majority of these stories haven't written down.
- The majority of these stories aren't written down. etc,

Errors in (10) may be attributed to the context of learning. Learners usually require a good grasp of learning of English tense, aspect, the modals and negation before different types of conditional sentences are introduced to them. English grammar text books provide only simplified information of this topic by introducing the three major types of conditional sentences and there are no sufficient exercises for them. Moreover, Kurd learners do not have enough information about the types of if clauses found in their language. Support to this, Mahwi is on the view that "the grammatical elements and materials of Kurdish language in the curriculum are not set according to results and outcomes of the linguistic studies." (Mahwi, 2/24/2008)[2]

Table 5.9. Errors with *do*

Production	FQ	Item	Recognition	FQ	Item
1. a. underuse of *do* as a main v. don't+^+comp//don't+do+comp.	33	1	1.ā. Underuse of do as an auxiliary verbs What+auxiliary verbs+s+^+comp// what+auxiliary verbs+s+inf+comp	7	1
b. Misunderstanding tense with *do*. Didn't do//don't do	29	1			
c. *be* misused with *do*.	4	1			
d. *have* misused with *do*.	1	1			
e. archi/ alternative forms.	47	1			
f. misformation of the next verbal word in emphatic. did+helped//did help	10	1			

Examples of such deviant structures are:

- *If you had gone to Kurdistan, you would learn Kurdish.
- *If you have gone to Kurdistan, you learn Kurdish.
- *If you were gone to Kurdistan, you will learn Kurdish.
- *If you went to Kurdistan, you have learned Kurdish.
- *If you have been gone to Kurdistan, you can learn Kurdish.
- *If you have gone to Kurdistan, you learn Kurdish.
- You would have gone to Kurdistan, you would learn Kurdish.
- *If you had gone to Kurdistan, you had learn Kurdish, etc.

Errors in (11) can be ascribed to approximation/communication strategy. Since *have* and *would like* are semantically equivalent (used to convey offer), learners tend to use them alternatively, probably as a result of forgetting the right form of the modal.

Another explanation of this error is due to the misanalysis. Learners consider the subjunctive form [bixorawa] which is used to convey the meaning for offer with a falling tone as the imperative [bixorawa] with a rising tone, since both verbs have the same form. They translate it to the imperative verb form *have*.

Morphologically, the verb in imperative mood in Kurdish is formed from the present stem with the prefix [b/bi] and ending with the person/ number suffixes /-a/ and/ø/ for singular and/-n/ for plural objects. The verb in this mood does not include any subject as in all languages, (Bomba, 2001:76). Similarly, Verbs in subjunctive mood are characterized by having the prefix

Table 5.10. Errors with *be*

Pro	FQ	item	Rec.	FQ	item
2. a. *be* omission. S¹+so+ ^+S² b. in passive O.+havenot+p.p,//O+havenot +been +p. p.	60 27	1 1	2. ā be omission ..^+going to+inf//be going to+inf.	27	1
3. addition /alternating other auxiliary verbs forms) S1+SO+any aux /be+S2	6	1			
4. misordering S1+so+S2 +be	2	1			
			5. lack of agreement I are not//I amnot	11	1
			6. overgeneralization I'm//I am	39	1

and the mood marker [b/bi] attached to the present stem followed by the pronominal suffixes. Verbs in subjunctive mood appear either alone or as an element in a large utterance.

5.2.1.4 Errors with the Modals

Errors shown in table 5.12 are those committed in the area of misuse of the modals. Errors in (12) can be attributed to false analogy. Students treat *dare* as a lexical verb since they negate it with the dummy *do*. It may be due to their faulty concepts hypothesized since they do not distinguish between the auxiliary *dare* and the lexical verb *dare to*. It may also be due to the context of learning, since grammar text books do not give enough practice to make learners distinguish between the two forms. Examples of such errors are:

- **Do they dare say he's coward?*

Errors in (13) (archi\alternating forms) are the product of achievement strategy/ a type of communicating strategy, which are activated when the "learner decides to keep the original communication goal but compensates for insufficient means or makes the effort to retrieve the required items", (Ellis, 1985: 180–182). Learners know that *dare* is an auxiliary since they do not use as an operator. Therefore, they use other auxiliary instead to convey the message. Examples of such errors are:

Table 5.11. Errors with *have*

Recognition	FQ	items	Production	FQ	Items
7. Misformation of past perfect aspect	115	1			
8. Misinformation	76	1			
9. Misformation of present perfect in negation	125	1			
10. Misunderstanding tense with modals(miscellaneous forms)	162	1	Should have// should	22	1
11. Alternating *have* with a modal	20	1			

- *can you dare say he is coward?*
- *are you dare say he is coward?*
- *does he dare say he is coward?*
- *shall you dare say he is coward?*
- *did you dare say he is coward?*
- *am you dare say he is coward?*

Errors of (14) may be attributed to avoidance strategy/syntactic avoidance. Learners try avoiding using the verb *dare* entirely. Instead of using the demanded auxiliary, they used (*is*) and form the interrogative erroneously. The example bellow is a sample of such a deviant form:

- *Is he coward?*

Or it may be due to the simplification strategy, which is exploited by the learner to ease the burden of learning.

Errors in (15) may be attributed to interference, since in Kurdish the temporal reference point of the main verb in the matrix clause is prior to the reference point of the verb in the embedded clause, i.e., there is no sequence of tense rule like English, (Ahmed: 2004:190) whereas in English the verb is back shifted in the indirect speech (as explained in chapter 3). An example of such a deviant structure is:

- *John said I can swim.*
- *John said he can swim.*

Errors in (16) are the outcome of communicative strategy/achievement type. The testees tend to produce the required item, i.e., form indirect speech,

Table 5.12. Errors with the Modals

Production errors	FQ	ITEMS
12. Addition(double marking) Do +s+ dare + inf.	41	1
13. archi/ alternate forms other auxiliary verbss+dare+inf	47	
14. underuse in interrogative (dare/ Is+s.+inf)	28	1
15. incorrect tense use in indirect speech S+nonbackshifted aux+inf.	85	1
16. archi\alternating forms s+alterating *could* by other modals+inf		1
17. alternating forms Do you like//would you like.? Prefer to be//would prefer to be	21	1
18. misformation of modals	24	1
19. archi/alternate forms for expressing preferences. Other modals+s+inf?	89	3
20. archi/alternate forms S+don't need to	51	2
21. misuse of can	67	1

by using inappropriate modal forms instead of *could*. The followings are samples of such error types:

- *John said he shall go swim.
- *John said he will swim.
- *John said he couldn't swim.
- *John said he shall swim.

Errors in (17.a) may be attributed to the adoption of approximation, which is one type of communication strategy. Since *do you like, I prefer to be* share semantic feature with *would you like* and *I would prefer* respectively, by which offers and preferences are expressed in English, the learners alternate them to achieve the goal. The following are examples of this sort:

- *Do you like to drink some coffee?
- I prefer to be a teacher.

Errors in (18) can be considered as the outcome of interference. In Kurdish offers can be expressed with verbs in the subjunctive mood *[kwpek qāwat bo benim?]*. Whereas in English this meaning is conveyed via the use of a modal verb: *would you like a cup of coffee?* In this case, negative transfer occurs which leads to errors. Moreover, it may be due to achievement strategy. As in:

- *shall I bring you a cup of coffee?
- *will I bring you a cup of coffee?
- *can I bring you a cup of coffee?
- *Please drink coffee.
- *Please, you can drink a coffee.
- *Could you please drink some coffee?

Errors in (19) can be attributed to communication strategy/ achievement type. The learner tries to express the preference meaning but he/she is not sure which auxiliary is used. In spite of his/ her ignorance of the target language rule, he/she tries to convey the meaning, but by the use of an alternative auxiliary. Examples of such deviant forms are:

- *I must be a teacher.
- *I would rather to be a teacher.
- *You will can be a teacher.
- *We ought to be a teacher.
- *I will become a teacher.

Errors in (20) can be attributed to misanalysis, since the subjects express the notion of non-necessity via the lexical form of *need,* i.e., *need to.* It may also be the outcome of approximation strategy, since the lexical *need to* and the auxiliary *need* convey the same meaning of necessity, learners tend to use it to express the meaning of non-necessity.

- *you don't need to buy a new one.

Errors in (21) may be the result of the context of learning, i.e., it is attributed to the way the modals are taught as a list according to the grammar text books, since *can* is introduced primarily to express permission, learners tend to overuse it in all situations because the patterns that have learned earlier have priority upon the patterns learned later. On the other hand, this sort of error may be attributed to culture issues and the effect of L1. In Kurdish, asking for permission is expressed mostly via the lexical verb [datwānim] followed by a verb in subjunctive mood, Bomba (2001:106 ff). So, learners translate this word to its equivalent [can] and overgeneralize it to English. Corder (1973: 289) argues that "errors may be due to overgeneralization derived from the characteristics of the mother tongue". Thus, they are unaware that in formal situations *may* is mostly used.

- *can I leave?

An explanation of such error-types that are shown in table 5.13 (22, a-b-c-d) can be attributed to overgeneralization / misformation category. Learners make these errors by false analogy to other classes of verbs in English such as (V be + ing), catenatives verbs which are followed by (to+ inf.) or to (have +p.p.) or (v + third person sg.s). It can be observed from the frequency table above that the frequency of errors of recognition is more than that of production. This fact has been stressed by applied linguists like Dulay, Burt and Krashen, (1982: 159) that "learners commonly make regularization errors in their comprehension of grammar", [regularization means overgeneralization].

Table 5.13. Errors with the Modals (continued).

Production	FQ	Item	Recognition	FQ	Item
22. misforming the modal					
a. modal+v+ed	8	6	a. amodal+v+ed	67	1
b. modal+v+ing	4	4	b. modal+v+ing	9	1
c. modal+v+ s	1	1	c. modal+s/3rd person	74	3
d. modal+to+inf//odal+inf	5	5	d. modal+be+inf//modal+ing	16	1

- *I can helped them.
- *I must helped them.
- *He can swum.
- *You needn't buying a new one.
- *I'd prefer being a teacher not a translator.
- *He can swims.

The error type in (23), which is shown in table 5.14 is also of overgeneralization/ additional category. Such errors occur in the later stages of L2 learning, when the learner has acquired some target language rules, (Dulay, Burt and Krashen, 1982: 159). They occur by false analogy to other regular verbs like (go, help . . . etc,) which take the third person singular *s*. In other words, since there are regular and irregular verbs in English, L2 learners tend to apply the regular rule to the modals in the same way. The outcome will be such deviant forms as:

Table 5.14. Errors with the Modals (continued)

Production	FQ	Item
23. Modal+s//modal (-s)	4	3
23. Modal+s//modal (-s)	4	3

- *She mays sleep.
- *He cans swim.

5.3.1.5 Be Redundancy

Such errors (24), which are presented in table 5.15, can be explained in terms of verbal collocation, since learners occasionally encounter these forms (will be, shall be, etc,) in the grammar text books and learning contexts. Examples of such errors are:

- *All the students must be go, only Azad can stay.
- *All the students must be go, only Azad can be stay.
- *All the students must be go, only Azad can stay.
- *All the students have to be go, only Azad can stay.
- *If you have going to Kurdistan, you will be learn Kurdish, etc.

Table 5.15. *be* Redundancy (errors with the modals).

Production	FQ	Item	Recognition	FQ	Item
24. modal+be+inf// modal+inf	23	4	24. modal+be+inf// modal+inf	16	1

It is noted that the testees translate [dabet] differently by *must, should, have to*. This is because modality is not taken as a topic in their Kurdish grammar lessons and that they only know such meanings through reading and listening.

Errors in (25, 26) in table 5.16 are of importance, though the frequency of their occurrence is low. It signals the fact that Kurd college learners have not mastered a number of patterns in English grammar, such as negative, interrogative, the position of frequency adverbs in terms of auxiliary (in recognition) and the way the modals are combined in a sequence. Examples of such erroneous forms are;

- *We can go?
- *He never would trust you.
- *I not need have gone to the office yesterday.
- *I will can to be a teacher.
- *You shall should not need to buy a new one.

Table 5.16. Errors with the Modals (Continued).

Production	FQ	Items	Recognition	FQ	Items
25. word order s+modal+inf?// moda+s+inf?	4 7 6	2 4 4	26. Word order s+not+modal+inf// s+modal+not+inf. S+adv.+modal+inf	24	5
26. auxiliary verbssequence s+modal+modal					

- *He don't need a new one. etc,

Moreover, the erroneous sentence (83) can be attributed to interference, since in Kurdish forming Yes-No question does not require subject-verb inversion but it is indicted by intonation. Similarly, the deformed sentence (85) may also be due to negative transfer. In Kurdish negation is made pre-verbally, i.e., any of the negative markers [nā, na, ma] are put before the main verb [such as in [nārom, nakait, maxo].

5.3.1.6 Mismatching of Auxiliary in Tag

Errors in (27.a), in table (5.17), may be due to context of learning of hyper-correction by the teachers. Since learners are usually reminded to use *do* as an operator in questions, so they tend to use it in positions where it does not require one. Errors in (27.b) may be due to non-mastery of forming tag questions in English, since the operator in the main sentence is *may*, they tend to use it in the tag questions, too. However, errors of (27.c) may be attributed to overgeneralization of the contraction rule in English. Since learners use the contracted forms of auxiliary in tag questions such as (isn't, aren't, won't, shan't, etc.), they overgeneralize that rule and apply it to may also, ignorance from its exception.

There are a number of errors that lie out of this grammatical taxonomy, such as:

Q3: (item 1):8erros=4%

- *Excuse me, today I want to go back early.
- *If you can give me a permission.
- *Could I have permission to leave?

Q3 :(item 2): 8errors= 4%

- *I conclude she has a later night.
- *I conclude she is sleepy.
- *I conclude she didn't sleep last night.

Table 5.17. Mismatching of Auxiliary in Tags

Recognition	FQ	Item
27. mismatching		
a. donot_+s?	23	1
b. may+s.?	34	1
c. mayn't + s?	7	1

Q3 :(item: 3) 28errors=15%

- *It isn't necessary to buy another.
- *That is not necessary to buy anew one.

Q3 :(item: 4) 11errors=6%

- *I want to offer you a cup of coffee.
- *Would you like to prepare some coffee for you?
- *Drink some coffee.
- *I will happy if you drink some coffee.

The above errors can be attributed to the use of circumculation strategy/ communication strategy. The learner does not recognize the real expressive form required, therefore he tries to describe the action by using another form.

Q4 (item: 3) 11errors=6%

- *I 'helped them. (stress)
- *I helped them surely.
- *I'm surely helped them.
- I insist I help them.

The above errors can be attributed to the interference, since in Kurdish emphatic is expressed by stress or lexically, i.e., by using such expressions like [ba dilniai, ba rasti, etc,]. So, the learner translates these words to L2. Research results show that negative language interference is the most noticeable source of error, often indicated by the translation similar they are similar in structure to a semantically equal phrase or sentence in the learners' first language, (Dulay, Burt and Krashen, 1982: 171).

Q5, (item 3):8 errors

- *Going? [bifoin]?
- *Leave?
- *Go?
- *Go away?
- The above errors are also attributed to interference. Since in Kurdish invitation is expressed via subjunctive verbs, i.e. auxiliary verbs are not used for this purpose, the learner translates [bifoin], which is a subjunctive verb, into such deviant forms faultily

The error types of the Q1 question reflect the testees' failure to recognize the exact meaning of the modal or they confuse different modal meanings, such as may for prediction which is confused for other distracters as follows;

5.3.1.7 Confusion between the Modal Meanings

Confusions of the modal meanings of this group of learners in the recognition level are illustrated in table 5.18.

Table 5.18. Confusion of Modal Meanings in the Recognition Level

The Modal	Correct Meaning	Confused With/	FQ	Confused With/	FQ	Confused With/	FQ
may	permission	prediction	27	necessity	17	obligation	14
can	possibility	ability	90	intention	22	willingness	16
Ought to	necessity	permission	8	possibility	15	ability	24
can	possibility	permission	5	prediction	52	obligation	20
must	prediction	intention	33	willingness	25	obligation	50
could	Past ability	Past permission	2	Past possibility	9	Past obligation	2
Supposed to	obligation	intention	53	insistence	39	ability	11
Be going to	prediction	intention	19	obligation	19	possibility	44
shall	intention	permission	11	possibility	27	necessity	81
Had to	willingness	necessity	56	possibility	33	insistence	44

Moreover there are other confusions of modal meanings in the production level as shown in table 5.19.

Since this group of errors is related to the semantic aspect of auxiliary, inferring their sources is not predictable. Corder (1973: 262) points out that "we rely rather heavily in our studies of errors on productive data", as failures in comprehension cannot be detected since in any act of comprehension there is a major component supplied by the situation and the hearer.

Despite the above fact, the above error types can be attributed to a number of factors:

The effect of L1; since there are no modal verbs in Kurdish but there are other means to express modality.

Table 5.19. Confusion of Modal Meanings in the Production Level

Prediction/suggestion	27	1 Q3(item2)
Prediction/possibility	34	1 Q3(item2)
Prediction/obligation	11	1 Q3(item2)
Non necessity/obligation	28	1 Q4(item3)

The meaning of the modals is also another source of confusion as each modal can have more than one meaning and each meaning is a member of an inter related system.

Moreover, in the testees responses there are (214, 3.218%) of unanswered items. They can be attributed to the adoption of avoidance strategy/ topic avoidance, in which the learner avoids answering the topic entirely.

NOTES

1. The Kurdish examples he provides include [xwārdwa, xwārdwa, etc], which are in fact present perfect in Kurdish rather than past perfect- a personal meeting with (Mahwi and Waria in 10/29/2007).
2. In a personal meeting with Mahwi.

Chapter Six

Conclusions, Pedagogical Recommendations and Suggestions for Further Research

6.1 CONCLUSIONS

In the light of the previous discussions related to the test findings, aims and hypothesis, the following conclusions have been drawn:

1. The majority of Kurd EFL university learners at the third stage encounter difficulties in recognizing and producing the syntactic and semantic aspects of English auxiliary verbs. This is reflected through their low performance in the main test, since the rate of their correct responses (43.38346%) is lower than the rate of their incorrect responses (56.61654%). These results validate the first hypothesis of the present study which states that: Most Kurd EFL university students do not often have full mastery of English auxiliary verbs.

2. At the recognition level, the findings of the data analysis for Q1 vs. Q2 show that the subjects' achievement is lower in recognizing the meanings of English auxiliary, i.e., the modals meanings) verbs than their achievement in recognizing the forms of these verbs. This is indicated by the rate of the correct responses to the first question (55%) which is lower than the rate of the correct responses to the second question (67%). These results verify the second hypothesis of the study which states: Kurd learners' ability in recognizing the forms of English auxiliaries is anticipated to be better than their ability in recognizing meanings of English auxiliaries. The same hypothesis is also validated by comparing the mean of the Q2 (127.8) which is higher than that of the Q1 (103.6).

3. Data analysis has also revealed that Kurd EFL learners encounter much more difficulty in producing English auxiliary verbs than in recognizing them. This is indicated by comparing the SD of Q1 and Q2 (recognition test) against Q3, Q4, and Q5 (production test). The subjects' performance at the recognition level has obtained a higher mean (115.7) against a lower mean of (38.0667) at the production level. This verifies the third hypothesis which reads as: the performance of Kurd EFL university students at the recognition level is anticipated to be better than their performance at the production.

4. Error analysis has yielded that the errors could be traced back to a number of possible reasons such as:

a. Communication strategies: When communicating their ideas in English, Kurd EFL learners may encounter difficulty because they do not have full mastery of the foreign language. In this case, they tend to use different kinds of communication strategies such as achievement strategies, circumculation, and literal translation. These errors constitute the majority of learners' errors.
b. Inter-lingual transfer: This sort of transfer takes place when the learner acquires the foreign language partially, which in turn encourages overgeneralization, incomplete application of rules, false concept hypothesized or misanalysis, and failure to learn conditions for rule application.
c. Context of learning: since English auxiliary verbs have not been given due attention in English grammar books in general and the subjects' text books in particular errors occur.
d. Intralingual transfer: when the rules of L2 are not familiar to the learners, they make use of the rules of their L1. This is indicated by translation as a general phenomenon. But the testees in this study try to avoid using such a process because the auxiliary verbs in their mother tongue are different from those found in English; therefore, their responses do not reflect the influence of their mother tongue.

5. The previous and the present studies indicate that EFL learners face difficulty at different stages with English auxiliary verbs, and that this tends to be much more serious at the production level than at the recognition level.

6.2 PEDAGOGICAL IMPLICATIONS

On the basis of the findings arrived at, the following pedagogical implications can be stated.

1. The reason behind Kurd learners' unfamiliarity with English auxiliary verbs is that the material as a whole is introduced to the students only once in their university studies (during the second year in the case of the subjects of the present study). The study results indicate that Kurd university learners are in need of a longer exposure to this topic. Therefore, it makes sense for syllabus designers to break the material into simple components and to proceed step by step, and with maximum recycling starting with introducing it from their first stage of university studies. Accordingly, the learner will have ample opportunity to work out the material so that by the time they are in the fourth class they will be familiar with it and errors would be minimized.
2. It is advisable that auxiliary verbs' forms and meanings be presented in a systematic way so that the learners get acquainted with the different forms of English auxiliaries, and the formal features of each category (primary and the modals) and that the meanings of the different modals are to be presented as a system rather than a list, different drills are to be provided with different meanings (epistemic, denotic and dynamic), strength and degrees of the modals to the extent they will be able to differentiate between modal verbs like can-be able to, can-may, should-had better, etc.

6.3 SUGGESTIONS FOR FURTHER RESEARCH

The following topics are suggested for further research in this area:

1. A study like this can be conducted to investigate the pragmatic aspect of the modal auxiliaries.
2. A comparative study to investigate the similarity and differences between English and Kurdish auxiliary verbs.
3. Another study can be conducted to investigate Kurd learners' mastery of English If Clause Types.

Appendix

THE TEST

This appendix includes the last version of the test; all the questions which are given to the testees as such are included after being submitted to the jury members.

Q1 Choose the most appropriate modal meaning indicated as A, B, C and D:

1. You may go.
   A. permission. B. prediction. C. necessity. D. obligation
2. He can't be working at this hour!
   A. ability. B. intention. C. possibility, D. willingness
3. You ought to vote in the next election.
   A. permission. B. necessity. C. possibility. D. ability
4. The road can be blocked.
   A. permission. B. prediction. C. obligation. D. possibility
5. The phone is ringing. That must be my sister.
   A. intention. B. willingness. C. prediction. D. obligation
6. When I was sixteen, I could run 10 kilometers.
   A. past permission. B. past ability. C. past possibility. D. past obligation.
7. You are not supposed to answer in this way.
   A. intention. B. obligation. C. insistence. D. ability.
8. It is going to rain tomorrow.
   A. intention. B. obligation. C. possibility. D. prediction.
9. We shall celebrate this very night.
   A. intention. B. permission. C. posibility. D. necessity.
10. Someone had to be the loser.

A. willingness. B. necessity. C. possibility. D. insistence.

Q2 Choose the correct answer.

1. Are you writing?
   A. No, I aren't. B. Yes, I am. C. Yes, I'm. D. No, I not.
2. What _____ on Saturdays?
   A. Ken usually does. B. does Ken usually do. C. does Ken usually. D. usually does Ken do.
3. Rose _____ to sing on Saturday.
   A. can. B. will. C. is going. D. shall.
4. Joan _____ play.
   A. going to. B. can. C. is going. D. can to.
5. He _____ you.
   A. never would trust. B. would never trust. C. never would trusts. D. would never trusts.
6. You don't look good today. I think you _____ see a doctor.
   A. should. B. should have. C. should be. D. should had.
7. What time _____ dinner?
   A. has John. B. John has. C. does John have. D. has John got.
8. Might he _____ your umbrella?
   A. borrow. B. to borrow. C. borrowing. D. borrows.
9. I _____ gone to the office yesterday.
   A. needn't have. B. not need have. C. need. D. needn't.
10. They may arrive today _____?
    A. mayn't they. B. may not they. C. may they. D. do they.

Q3. What would you say in each of the following situations, use an appropriate modal verb?

1. You are speaking to Mr. Ari, who is one of your teachers. You want to leave class early today.
2. Nancy is yawning. What do you conclude (predict)?
3. A friend of yours bought a new suit yesterday. He wants to buy a new one today. You see it is not necessary for him to do so.
4. Offer your guest some coffee.
5. You prefer to be a teacher than a translator.

Q4 Do as you required by the instruction given between brackets:

1. They do their jobs. (Change into negative).
2. Alan is going to school. His brother is going to school, too. (Combine with so).
3. I helped them. (Make the verb emphatic).

4. I dare say he is coward. (Change into interrogative)
5. John said, "I can swim." (Change into indirect speech, John said...)

Q5 Translate the following sentences into English.

1. kātek min gaištim ,miwanakān ŕoištbūn.
2. hamw xwendikārakān dabet biŕon, tanhā āzād datwānet bimenetawa.
3. biŕoin?
4. zorbai zorī am ĉirokāna nanûsrāwinatawa. agar bíĉûytāyata kurdistān,ferī kurdī dabwit.

Bibliography

Alexander, L.G. (1988) *Longman English Grammar*, London: Longman.
Abdul Wahid, A. A. (1982) *Modality in English: a Semantic Study with Pedagogical Orientation*. MA Thesis. Basra: University of Basra.
Ahmed, M. F. (1988) *Kār Tawāw Kirdin la Kurdidā [verb complement in Kurdish]*. MA Thesis. University of Sulaimani.
——— (2004) *The Tense and Aspect System in Kurdish*. Unpublished Ph.D. Dissertation: University of London.
Anderson, D. S. (2006) *Auxiliaries and Auxiliary Verb Constructions*. www.ingentaconnect.com/content/oso/1764122/2006/00000001/00000001/art00001;jsessionid=6vvg91c49o69f.alexandra
Amin, W. O. (1979). *Aspects of the Verbal Construction in Kurdish*. Unpublished Ph.D. Dissertation. University of London.
Alānī, R.A. (1985) "Kāri habûn" [Verb of habûn]. In *Karwa*. ed. Muslih Mustafa Jalali. NO. (29), pp15–19. Baghdad: dār āfāq Arabia.
Ali Amin, N. (1986) "Ĉāwgī Bun w Habûn la Zimani Kurdidā" [the inf. of habûn and bûn in Kurdish language]. In *Rošinbiri Nwe–* ed. Muslih Mustafa Jalali, NO. (109) pp: 229–245. Baghdad: Dar Al-Huria.
Ahmed, B.O. (2005) *Darbŕīnī Reža la Diālektī Žwrûi Zimāni Kûrdidā [expressing mood in Northern dialect of Kurdish]* Unpublished Ph.D. Dissertation. University of Saladin.
Ali Abdul Amir, A.M. (2006) *Investigating Iraqi EFL University Students' Performance in Using Weak Forms*. Unpublished MA Thesis. University of Babylon.
AlMousawi, S. K. (2006*) Investigating The Difficulties Faced By Iraqi EFL University Learners in Using Transitional Conjuncts*. Unpublished MA Thesis. University of Babylon.
Baker, D. (1989) *Language Testing*. London: Edward Arnold.
Brown Douglas, H. (1994) *Principles of Language Learning And Teaching*. New Jersey: Prentice Company.
Bachman, L. F. (1990) *Fundamental Considerations in Language Testing*. Oxford: Oxford University Press.
Brown, H. D. (1987) *Principles of Language Learning and Teaching* (second edition). New Jersey: Prentice Hall Regents, Englewood Cliffs.
Baban, S. (1997) *Mikānizma Binaŕatiakāni RistaSāzi Rezmānī bûn w habûn* (fundamental mechanisms of [bûn] and [habûn]) Hawler: University Of Saladin.
Baban, S. (1997) *Dainamizmi Jenawi Likaw la Rista Sazida(the dynamism of personal pronouns in syntax)*. Hawler: Mardin.

Bomba, R.M. (2001) *Kirdārī Îlzāmī (wist w ārazw) la Zimāni Kurdidā-Diālectī Kirmānjī Nāwrast [the subjunctive verb in Kurdish –in the central dialect]*. MA Thesis, University of Sulaimani.
Blanco, H. A. (2002) *The Rise of Modal Meanings in Early Modern English*.UniversidadDeSantiagodialnet.unirioja.e/sservlet/fichero_articulo?codigo=1700552& orden=60688.
Chandra Bose, A. (2005). *The Problems in Learning Modal Auxiliary Verbs in English at High School Level*, unpublished Ph. D. Dissertation, http: //www. languageinIndia.com/nov2005/chandrabosee1.html
Cowie, et al (1989) *Oxford Advanced Learner's Dictionary* (Fourth Edition). Oxford: Oxford University Press.
Cohen and Dörnyei (170–185), (2002) *An Introduction to Applied Linguistics*. Edited by Schmitt, N. London: Arnold.
Celece-Murcia, M. and Larsern- Freemen, D. (1999) *The Grammar Book*. Boston: Heinle and Heinle.
Crystal, D. (1992). *An Encyclopedic Dictionary of Language and Languages*. UK: Blackwell.
(2003) *The Cambridge Encyclopedia of the English Language*. (Second edition). New York: Cambridge University Press.
Cook, V. J. and Newson, M., (1996) *Chomsky's Universal Grammar*.UK: Blackwell Publishers.
Corder, S. P. (1973) *Introducing Applied Linguistics*. United Kingdom, Australia: Penguin Education.
Cohen, Andrew, D. (1996) *Second Language Learning and Use Strategies: Clarifying Issues*, www.carla.umn.edu/about/profiles/CohenPapers/SBIclarify.pdf
Dulay, H. (1982) *Applied Linguistics*. Oxford: Oxford University Press.
Dahl, O. (1985) *Tense and Aspect Systems*. US: Basil Blackwell.
Dulay, H. M. Burt, and S. Krashen, (1982) *Language Two*. New York: Oxford University Press.
Dizaïy, O. (1984) "Barawrd Kirdneki 'Rabwrdwi Tawaw'i Kurdi lagal 'Perfect'i zimana Awrupiakanda". *[A comparative of past perfect of Kurdish with the European languages]*. In *Karwan,* ed. Muhammad Amin Muhammad Ahmed – NO (24). Baghdad: dār āfāq Arabia.
Ellis, R. (1985) *Understanding Second Language Acquisition*. Oxford: Oxford University Press.
Eckersley, C.E. and Eckersley, J. M. (1960) *A Comprehensive English Grammar*. England: Longman.
Farhady, H. Jafrpoor, A. and Birjandi, P. (1995) *Testing Language Skills from Theory to Practice*. Tehran: The Centre of Studying and Compiling.
Finch, G. (2000) *Linguistic Terms and Concepts*. London: Macmillan.
Fries, C.C. (1952) *The Structure of English*. London: Longman, Green.
Fromkin, V.; Rodman, R.; Hyams, N. (2003) *An Introduction to Language*. United Kingdom, Thomson Heinle.
Fintel Von K. (2006) *Modality and Language*.http://semantics-online.org/fintel
Fakhri, N. and Mukiriani, K. (1982) *Rezmani Kurdi bo Polī Yakamī Baši Zimanī Kurdī Zankoi Salahaddin[Kurdish grammar for the first year studies in the department of kurdish, University of Saladin]*. Hawler: University of Saladin.
Faxri, N. M. (1994) "Firmāni Yāridadar Ĉia W?Bo Ĉiw Kai W? Ĉi Dagaianet la Zimani Kurdida?" [What is an auxiliary verb in Kurdish? When and why it is used? And what does it mean in Kurdish?]. In *Rošinbiri Nwe, ed.* Muslim Mustafa Jalali – NO (136). pp. (32–40). Baghdad: dār al-Huria.
Faxri, N. M. (1996) "Yarmati Dari Firman Xaleki Piršingdara la Kaseti Zimānī Kurdidā Ĉon W Bo?" [verbal auxiliary is a bright point in the personality of Kurdish language, how and why?] In *Rošinbiri New,* ed. Muslim Mustafa Jalali – NO (138) pp. (10–16).Baghdad: Dar al –Huria.
Gramley, S. and Pätzold Kurt Michael, (2004) *A Survey of Modern English* (second edition). London and New York: Routledge.
Grover, H. (2000) *Essential Introductory Linguistics*. USA: Blackwell Publishers.

Guasti, M. T. (2002) *Language Acquisition*. England: Cambridge, Massachusetts.
Graver, B.D. (1986) *Advanced English Practice*. Oxford: Oxford University Press.
Huddleston, R. and Pullum Geoffrey K. (2002) *The Cambridge Grammar of the English Language*. Cambridge: Cambridge University Press.
Harris, D. P. (1969) *Testing English as a Second Language*. New York: McGraw-Hill Book Company.
Hughes, A. (2003) *Testing For Language Teachers*. Cambridge: Cambridge University Press.
Haspelmath, M. (2002) *Understanding Morphology*. London: Arnold.
Heaton, J.B. (1988) *Writing English Language Tests*. New York: Longman Group UK Limited.
Hawramani, A.M. (1981) *Zārī Zimāni Kurdī la Tirāzwi Barāwirdā*.[Kurdish dialect in the comparison balance]. Iraq: Baghdad: dar al tiba'a wal nashir
Harris, C. McLaughlin, B. Still, M. (ND) *Modals: A Balancing Ac* .http://www2.gsu.edu/~wwwesl/issuel/modaltoc.htm.pp.1–5
Johnson, K. and Johnson, H. (1999) *Encyclopedic Dictionary of Applied Linguistics*. Oxford: Blackwell Publishers.
Kuiper, K. and Allan W. Scott, (1996) *An Introduction to English Language*. London: Macmillan Press Ltd.
Kurdoev, K .K. (1982) *Rezmāni Kurdi ba Karastai Diālekti Kirmānjī Soranī* (Kurdish grammar with reference to kurmanji dialects, translated by Mukiriani. from Russian). Al-adib: Baghdad.
Kim, Yoon- Kyu, (2006) "Why Are Some Language Learners More Successful Than Others?" Korea Military Academy: ALAK newsletterwww.alak.or.kr/2_public/2006_fall/Include/f1.pdf.
Kusutani, S. (ND) "The English Copula Be: Japanese Learners' Confusion", web1.hpu.edu/images/.../TESL_WPS/04Kusutani_Syntax_a17235.
Krashen, S. (1981) *Second Language Acquisition and Second Language Learning*. University of Southern California: Pergamon Press.
Keshaverz, M. H. (2004) *Contrastive Analysis and Error Analysis*. Tehran: Rahnama Publications.
Lado, R. (1964) *Language Teaching*. London: McGraw-Hill.
────── (1961) *Language Testing. The Construction and Use of Foreign Language Tests*. London: Longman.
Leech, G. and Svartvic, J. (1994) *A Communicative Grammar of English*. London: Longman.
Leech, G. (1971) *Meaning and the English Verb*. London: Longman.
────── (1969) *Towards a Semantic Description of English*. London: Longman.
Lewis, M. (2002) *The English Verb*. USA: Heinle, Thomson.
Mackey A. and Gass, S. M. (2005) *Second Language Research*. London: Lawrence Erlbaum Associates Publishers.
Madsen, H.S. (1983) *Techniques in Testing*. Oxford: Oxford University Press.
Major, R. C. and Kim, E. (1996) "The Similarity Differential Rate Hypothesis". *Language Learning* VOL. 46, no.3 pp.465–496.
McLaughlin, B. (1987) *Theories of Second Language Learning*. London: Edward Arnold.
Mitchell, R. and Myles, F. (2004) *Second Language Learning Theories*. London: Arnold.
McCarus, E. N. (1958) *A Kurdish Grammar* (Descriptive Analysis of the Kurdish of Sulaimani, Iraq). New York: American Council of Learned Societies.
Mousavi, S.A. (1999) *A Dictionary of Language Testing* (Second Edition). Iran: Rahnama Publications.
Mahwi, M. (2001) *Ristasāzī Kurdī (Kurdish syntax)*. University of Sulaimani: Sulaimani.
Muhammad, M. (1974) *Wird Būnawa la Ĉand Bāseki Rezmānī Kurd [examining some matters of Kurdish grammar]*. kori zaniari kurd.Kurdī; Baghdad.
Marif, A. (2000) *Rezimānī Kurdi*. bargi yakam(wisha sazi) basi pencam(kirdar), [Kurdish grammar: fist volume : chapter five (verb)]: Sulaimani: Sardam.
────── (1992). "Kirdari Yaridadar la Zimani Kurdida" [Auxiliary verbs in Kurdish]. In *Rošinbiri New*, ed. Muslih Mustafa Jalali. NO. (129) pp 9–17. Baghdad: dar al -huria.
Musa, A.KH. (2000) *Rezmani Bûn w Habûn la Kurdida (the Grammar of bun and habûn in Kurdish)*. Unpublished MA Thesis: University of Saladin.

Mohamed A. R. Li Lian, G. Eliza W.R. (2004) "English Errors and Chinese Learners". *Sunway College Journal* 1, 83–97 (2004)
Ma'ruf, M. F. (1989) "Kār Pollen Kirdin ba Pei Ronān"*[verbal classification in terms of inflection]*. In *Rošinbiri New,* ed. Muslih Mustafa Jalali .No (121) pp.(40–58). Baghdad: Dar Al-Huria liltiba'a.
Mackenzie, D. N. (1961) *Kurdish Dialect Studies*. London: Oxford University Press.
Nabaz, J.(1976*) zimani yakgirtwi Kurdi(towards ā unified Kurdish language)*. Germany: Bamberg.
Navarro, L. Q. R. (2002) *"Verb Phrases and Noun Phrases in English"*. University of Granada. http//www.google.com
Oanh and Hein, (2006) "Memorization and EFL Students' Strategies at University Level In Vietnam". Journal of 'TESL-EJ' Teaching English as a second language or foreign language. Volume 10, NO.2. From http//www.google.com.
Palmer, F., (1971) *Grammar*. England: Longman.
Payne, T.E. (1997) *Describing Morphosyntax*. Cambridge: Cambridge University Press.
Quirk, R. and Greenbaum, S. (1990) *A Students Grammar of the English Language*. England: Longman.
Quirk, R. Greenbaum, S. Leech, G. Svartvic, J. (1985) *A Comprehensive Grammar of the English Language*. London: Longman.
Roberts, P. (1956) *Patterns of English*. New York. Harcourt, Brace, and World, Inc.
Radford, A. (1997) *Syntax*. New York: Harcourt, Brace and the World.
Radford, A. (1988) *Transformational grammar*. UK: Cambridge University Press.
Rasūl, Zs ,(2006) *Rista Sazi W Wata Sazi (Bun) (the syntax and semantics of bûn)*. Unpublished MA thesis.
Staggerberg, Norman C. (1971) *An Introductory English Grammar*. New York: Holt, Reinhart and Winston.
Spolsky, B. (1989) *Conditions for Second Language Learning*. Oxford: Oxford University Press.
Show, H. (1986) *Mc Graw-Hill Handbook of English*. New York: McGraw-Hill Book Company.
Shwāni, R. M. (2003) *Āmrazi Bastinawa La Zimani Kurdidā (relative articles in kurdish)*. Unpublished Ph. D. Dissertation. Sulaimani: Sardam.
Soane, E. B. (1913) *Grammar of the Kurmanji or Kurdish Language*. London: LUZAC &CO.
Shihab, S. S. (1984) *Analysis of Errors Made By Iraqi Students in Secondary Schools in the Area of the English Verb Phrase*. Unpublished MA Thesis, University of Basra.
Thomson, A.J. and Martinet, A.V. (1986*) A Practical English Grammar*. Oxford: Oxford University Press.
Trask, R. L. (1993) *A Dictionary of Grammatical Terms*. London and New York: Routledge.
Thornborrow .J. and Wareing, S. (1998) *Patterns in Language*; *an introduction to language and literary style*. London and New York: Routledge.
Tallerman, M. (1998*) Understanding Syntax*. London: Arnold.
Whitehoall. (1956) *Structural Essentials of English*. London: Longmans, Green.
Thompson Michael., (2002) "Modals in English Language Teaching". Italy. www3.telus.net/linguisticsissues/modalsinteaching.html - 29k
Thackston, W. M. 2006. *Sorani Kurdish-A Reference Grammar with Selected Readings* http://www.fas.harvard.edu/~iranian/sorani/index.html.
Widdowson, H. G. (1990) *Aspects of Language Teaching*. Oxford: OUP.
Weir, C. J. (1990) *Communicative Language Testing*. New York: Prentice Hall.
Wahbi, T. (1929) *Dasturi Zmani Kurdi* (jizmi yakam)[Patterns of Kurdish Language]. Baghdad:Dar al-tiba'a al-haditha.
Wouden, T.vd.(1966) *Three Modal Verbs*.www.let.rug.nl/~vdwouden/docs/modhist2.pf
Yule, G. (1996) *The Study of Language*. UK: CUP.
Yosopova (1987). "Kar" [verb]. In *Rošinbiri Nwe,* ed. Muslih Mustafa Jalali–NO. (116), pp.71–9. Baghdad: dar al- huria

INTERVIEWS

Meetings with Dr. Muhammad Mahwi/ four times every month.
Meeting with Runak M. Bomba.
Meeting with Waria Amin.

About the Author

Paiman was born in Hallabja, a city in the north of Iraq. There, she completed her secondary school study, but later moved to Sulaimani. She got her BA in English Language and Literature in Mosul University and her MA in Linguistics/Applied Linguistics at the University of Sulaimani.

Paiman taught EFL students in secondary schools and Teachers institute. When she got her MA, she worked as the assistant of the head of English department for three years, and currently she is teaching different subjects in this department, such as Linguistics, Syntax grammar, cross culture and Morphology, supervising and working as a researcher at the College of Basic Education.

Since 2013 she has published four studies in the field of Applied Linguistics, and is currently working on two new studies.

The author is interested in attending conferences and workshops; she read her three papers in different conferences. In 2012 she read a paper on "The Use of Language Games in Language Learning" in KELTPN organization, another paper which was also published in the 5th international conference at ISHK university in 2014 entitles "Acquisition and Learning", furthermore her third paper which entitles "Borrowing, the outcome of language contact" read by her and got publication confirmation in the first international conference in UHD university.

The author got Fulbright scholarship in USA at Salem State University/ MA and could get that certificate successfully in 2014.

www.ingramcontent.com/pod-product-compliance
Lightning Source LLC
Chambersburg PA
CBHW020749230426
43665CB00009B/552